Corporate Chanakya on Management

Corporate Chanakya on Management

INCLUDES AUDIOBOOK READ BY TOM ALTER

SPMGROUP
SINCE 1967
SPM Foundation

Radhakrishnan Pillai

JAICO PUBLISHING HOUSE

Ahmedabad Bangalore Chennai
Delhi Hyderabad Kolkata Mumbai

Published by Jaico Publishing House
A-2 Jash Chambers, 7-A Sir Phirozshah Mehta Road
Fort, Mumbai - 400 001
jaicopub@jaicobooks.com
www.jaicobooks.com

CORPORATE CHANAKYA ON MANAGEMENT
With Audiobook
ISBN 978-81-8495-342-8

First Jaico Impression: 2012
11th Jaico Impression: 2024

Printed by
Rashmi Graphics, Mumbai

The book is dedicated to
My Gurudev Swami Chinmayananda,
who inspired me to study our ancient scriptures that
offer solutions to all our modern day problems.

Contents

Author's Note

The journey of *Corporate Chanakya* has been encouraging beyond belief. For a debut author, writing the first book itself was a challenge. But seeing it grow into a national bestseller has been more than a dream come true! The team at Jaico did a fantastic job of publishing and distributing the book.

As a leadership trainer, I have been travelling across the globe teaching at various universities, business schools, corporates and government organisations. The media consistently carried fantastic reviews for the book. It has been heartening to always see it on the 'Most Recommended' or 'Best Sellers' shelves in bookshops.

Inspired by the book, Shemaroo, the entertainment company made *Chanakya Speaks*, an 'edutainment' film now ready for launch. It is the world's first business management film on Chanakya. During the making of the film, Shemaroo came up with the idea — an audio book on *Corporate Chanakya.*

Tom Alter, the veteran Bollywood actor and theatre and television artist, agreed to do the voice over. I am personally thankful to him for taking the book to another level altogether.

The book *Corporate Chanakya* had 3 sections – Leadership, Management and Training. During one of my training programmes, the Chairman of the company who was attending the program said, "Your book has 3 books within it!" I discussed the possibilities with Jaico, of bringing out *Corporate Chanakya* as 3 individual books on Leadership, Management and Training. And about giving voice to each of them!

So here you have in your hands *Corporate Chanakya on Management*, a single volume containing 70 chapters. And it comes along with an audio CD book that you can listen to, as you read! I highly recommend both, because revision only makes a student perfect. But do not forget to apply what you have learnt! Practise the theory. Act on the ideas. Implement your plan...

An Overview:

• Chanakya, Kautilya, and Vishnugupta are the names of the same person. Either of the names has been used in this book to refer to Chanakya.

• This book does not compare Indian management ideas against western management ideas. In fact it is complementary to western management thoughts. We have taken the best of both worlds.

• In most cases, leaders have been referred to as 'he'. But it also applies to 'she' as well. Since Chanakya has taken the King (male gender) as the leader, the pronoun 'he' is used. Leadership and management skills are not gender-based but they are qualities which can be developed as a 'mind-set'.

• In this book, I have referred to verses or *sutras* from *Kautilya's Arthashastra.* For those who would like to read the verse in the original text, the verse number is written in brackets. The first digit is the book number. The second is the chapter number and the third digit is the verse number. For example,

"He (leader) should constantly hold an inspection of their works, men being inconstant in their minds." (2.9.3)

So, this verse is from *Kautilya's Arthashastra* Book 2, Chapter 9 and Verse 3. The same format has been followed in all chapters.

• The book that readers can refer to for the verses quoted, is the English translation of *Kautilya's Arthashastra* by R.P. Kangle of Mumbai University, published by Motilal Banarasidas. The explanations given are the interpretation of the author. Various other translations and commentaries of *Arthashastra* other than this book are available.

TIP

This book has 70 chapters. The idea is not to read it as a novel but to enjoy its practical benefits. Read a chapter, or a few chapters, a day, apply the teachings in your life, and observe the benefits. It only takes three minutes to read each chapter.

Go ahead – Discover the Chanakya in you!

Preface

LET ME TELL you a story…

There was once a young man in Mumbai who wanted nothing more than to succeed in the world of business. He had studied management in colleges that extolled the virtues of the western ways of understanding this subject. Soon enough, he worked his way up the corporate ladder, but finally decided to set out on his own. After all, who wants to be bossed over by someone else?

His first venture was in the realm of spiritual tourism. Since no one in his family had ever been an entrepreneur, he had to learn everything about setting up a business on his own. By the grace of God, and the support of his business partner, the business began to do well. From being a manager in someone else's company, he had become the leader of his own business.

His next step? Creating a well-known corporate entity. He met people and discussed his ideas and plans with them, learning from people, making copious notes, reading books, attending seminars, and training programmes. And yet, nothing helped. Something vital was missing in his pursuit for knowledge. He was not able to figure out what this missing piece was, for a long time.

The answer was right within him.

Since his childhood, he had found guidance in a spiritual organisation and had been blessed by many spiritual masters. During a spiritual discourse a Mahatma said, "India, our motherland, has great history and legacy. Our *Rishis* were no ordinary men — they have studied and perfected every science in this world. Only if we were to look back into our glorious past we would find solutions to all our modern problems."

This was the divine message he had been waiting for.

Management has been recognised as a science since the 1950s. One of the fathers of modern management is Peter Drucker. But didn't 'management' exist in India even before the 1950s and the Drucker era? As a nation we have over 5000 years to our credit. Did we not have management scientists in our country before the 20th century?

In the ancient Indian scriptures — *Ramayana*, *Mahabharata*, the various *Upanishads* — he found brilliant discussions of management strategies. Why was it that we Indians, always look at what is *wrong* with India and never appreciate what is *great* about our country? As a nation we have survived the test of time. Even though we are still a growing economy, we are not a failed nation. In the past, our country had achieved the peak of success for thousands of years. How many nations can boast of such a heritage?

He now realised that the missing piece which would help his business grow was to look 'within' rather than outside. The western principles of management are undoubtedly good, but even his own ancestors were extremely good at management.

Thus, one day, while looking for Indian books on management, he stumbled upon *Kautilya's Arthashastra*, written by the kingmaker, Chanakya. Who has not heard about this book? Even he had. But hardly anyone from his generation had studied it. He bought a copy.

A few pages into the book, he was upset! He could not understand anything! He read the pages over and over again, but the message of the book was out of reach. The subject itself seemed dry and boring. He felt the author had made everything seem more complicated than necessary.

He said to one of his mentors, "I do not understand anything in the *Arthashastra*, even though I am trying my best to learn from it." His mentor told him, "In India, we consider the scriptures to be mirrors. They reflect who you are. So if you do not understand *Arthashastra*, do not blame the mirror. As you grow and experience life, you will understand the book better."

That year, he went on a pilgrimage to Kailash Mansarovar, the holy abode of Lord Shiva. One evening, a voice seemed to speak to him, 'Make *Kautilya's Arthashastra* your lifelong pursuit. Don't just study it, but apply it in your life. Live the *Arthashastra*!' He could not believe that he was listening to his *own* thoughts, this had to be divine intervention!

He had heard about an ashram in Kerala, dedicated to the

research of ancient Indian scriptures. He declared to the Acharya (teacher) in charge of the ashram, "I want to study the *Arthashastra*." The Acharya was happy to see the young man's interest, but said, "You will have to come here and learn it under the Guru-Shishya Parampara." This meant taking a break from the business and staying in the ashram and studying under a Sanskrit scholar.

This was not an easy decision for a businessman from Mumbai. But, with the help of his partner, he took time off from the business, and studied the wisdom of the Rishis. The time he spent in the ashram changed his life forever.

He realised that each modern management theory had already been explored thousands of years ago in the *Arthashastra*.

With a deeper knowledge of management he now returned to his urban life to apply what he had learned. Immediately, he experienced success! His business grew and people were impressed with his new skills. When they asked him how he had achieved success, he said, "Two things helped me — the grace of my Guru and the knowledge of *Kautilya's Arthashastra*."

Friends, this is my story. Every word is true. But, the story does not end here. In fact, this is where the story begins....

After I returned from Kerala I applied Kautilya's practical and perfect theories to my own business (Atma Darshan, *www.atmadarshan.com*). Even though Atma Darshan brought me success, something else began to happen. My friends from the corporate world urged me to share this knowledge I had gained.

I was invited to speak at various seminars, conferences, and training programmes in India and all over the world. Businessmen consulted me on several matters. Well-known publishing houses and newspapers asked me to write about how Kautilya's wisdom could be applied to modern businesses. I was also asked to host a radio show.

I met so many people who are interested in Indian management and Indian wisdom. Despite the differences between them with regard to age, nationalities, designations, and industries, all those who participated in my workshops and chose to attend my seminars felt a deep respect for Chanakya's genius.

And then came the support of the SPM Group of companies which allowed me to delve deeper into *Arthashastra*. I am now fully devoted to the cause of the promotion and application of Indian management ideas. Today, I am the Director of the SPM Foundation which aims to 'make India strong and self-sufficient' in the ancient Guru–Sishya Parampara method.

This book is a documentation of all my ideas that I have shared with millions of people from the corporate world, all across the globe, about how to apply Chanakya's practical solutions to solve day-to-day problems in modern businesses.

Corporate Chanakya on Management is not just about me. It's about you and everyone else who wants to practise the principles of Indian Management in their work and wants to be successful.

Chanakya
Who Was He?

BORN IN 4TH CENTURY B.C. in India, Chanakya was also known as Vishnugupta and Kautilya. Through the centuries, scholars have described Chanakya as a rare mastermind who became an expert in varied and specialised fields like management, economics, politics, law, leadership, governance, warfare, military tactics, accounting systems, and several others. The 6000 *sutras* have been classified into 15 books, 150 chapters, and 180 topics by Chanakya himself.

He was responsible for bringing down the Nanda dynasty and establishing his able student Chandragupta Maurya on the throne as the Emperor. Hence, he is called a 'Kingmaker'. He is also credited with masterminding the defeat of Alexander in India who was on his march to conquer the world.

As a political thinker, he was the first to visualise the concept of a 'nation' for the first time in human history.

During his time, India was split into various kingdoms. He brought them all together under one central governance, thus creating a nation called 'Aryavartha', which later became India. He documented his lifelong work in his book *Kautilya's Arthashastra* and *Chanakya Niti*.

For ages, rulers across the world have referred to the *Arthashastra* for building a nation on sound economics, based on spiritual values.

Arthashastra when literally translated means 'scripture of wealth' but it contains knowledge about every subject under the sun. It's the knowledge of wealth and a wealth of knowledge.

Acknowledgements

WHEN I STARTED on my journey to learn and teach Chanakya's ideas I was not sure about how it would work. It was just an idea, a dream. I took my first step and then thousands of well-wishers joined me and encouraged me along. The number of people who are responsible for making this book a reality is endless. I must acknowledge some of these wonderful people who gave me strength right from the start.

Chinmaya Mission

I am a 'product' of the spiritual organisation Chinmaya Mission (*www.chinmayamission.com*). I met my Gurudev Swami Chinmayananda (1916-1993) when I was a child. He is my spiritual and management guru. Gurudev said, "A single ideal can transform a listless soul into a towering leader among men." This statement has been the guiding principle of my life.

Today, Swami Tejomayananda, the global head of Chinmaya Mission, continues to give me the same support. He chose the beautiful name of my first company — Atma Darshan (vision of the self).

Among hundreds of Acharyas (teachers) of the mission, some with whom I am closely associated require mention — Swami Sacchidananda, Swami Sadananda, Swami Ishwarananda, Swami Swaroopananda, Swami Mitrananda, have encouraged me to spread the work of Chanakya.

Swami Advayanandaji — the Acharya in charge of Chinmaya International Foundation (CIF) accepted me as a student of CIF where I learnt the complete 6000 *sutras* of *Arthashastra* and this has been the turning point in my life.

Dr. Gangadharan Nair, former Dean of Adi-Shankara Sanskrit University, Kalady, Kerala, my teacher and my guru of *Arthashastra*. His wife, Dr. Uma Devi Nair, herself a Sanskrit scholar, was like a mother to me while I was studying the *Arthashastra*.

Venkat Iyer, my friend since childhood and later my partner in the company Atma Darshan. Without his support, I couldn't have spent time learning about Chanakya's work. He also runs a successful venture called Wealth Tree Partners (*www. wealthtree.in*).

Muulraj Chheda and SPM Group, came as a godsend. Muulraj, is the Director of Swati Energy and Projects Private Ltd, part of the SPM group of companies. SPM stands for Strength, Progress with Maturity, and is also the initials of the three Founder brothers — Shantilal, Pravin, and Mavji Chheda. They supported my research and promotion of Chanakya's works.

Today, I am the Director of SPM Foundation (*www. spmfoundation.in*) the education wing of SPM Group (*www. spmgroup.co.in*) the vision of which is to bring back ancient Indian knowledge and apply it to our modern day problems. The other directors of the SPM Group — Rajen Chheda, Kinnjal Chheda, Niket Shah, Guruvinder — and their spouses have supported me in my search of knowledge. Each day, when we sit for lunch together, I call it my 'classroom' where words of wisdom from senior members have always given me insights into the intricacies of human nature.

MTHR Global, is More Than HR Global (*www.mthrglobal.com*). The core team — Rajesh Kamath, Vipul Agarwal, Ashish Gakrey, Rajesh Gupta, and Preeti Malhotra — were the first to christen me *Corporate Chanakya*. I dedicate the title of this book to them.

Mumbai University's Dr. Shubhada Joshi, Head of Department of Philosophy, and her team, gave my work on Chanakya the academic outlook it required. SPM Foundation partnered with the Mumbai University for offering joint programmes on 'Chanakya's Management Ideas and Indian Philosophy'.

Worldspace Satellite Radio's Karthik Vaidyanathan, Harish Puppala, Seetal Iyer came up with a wonderful idea for a show called 'Ask Chanakya' on Moksha, a channel on Worldspace. I hosted at least a hundred shows.

Also, I am grateful to my other 'media friends' — Dinesh Narayan, Meenal Bhaghel, and William Charles D'Souza for their support.

Gautam Sachdev promoter of (*www.indiayogi.com*) introduced my first online e-course based on *Arthashastra*.

My course now has students from over 25 different countries. I am glad that I can use technology to take Chanakya's message to the world.

Several Management Gurus supported my thirst for knowledge. I would like to thank Dr. Subhash Sharma, Dr. M.B. Athreya, Debra and William Miller, Sudhir Seth, and Dr. Anil Naik.

I am grateful to the Police Force — Sandeep Karnik, (IPS) Dhanraj Vanzari, Milind Bharambe (IPS), Satish Menon (Railway Protection Force) — who made me realise that behind the tough looking cop there is a human being who feels just like you and me.

My family, especially my parents, C.K.K. Pillai and Sushila Pillai, have my heartfelt gratitude. Coming home late at night, not being sure of a regular income while I developed a business, missing weekends and family time while prioritising professional commitments, my life would never have been smooth without my wife Surekha. Her parents Shekhar and Dhanvati, and her sisters Sarikha and Chandrika bring joy to my life.

My First students of Arthashastra — Mala Thevar, Yogesh Sanghani, Anuraag Gupta, and his sister Seema Gupta, and Anupam Acharya. Their dedication to knowledge has given me the confidence that this good work will continue for many long years after I am gone.

And I must thank Ranjit Shetty, my friend from the Chinmaya Mission, who has decided to dedicate all his time to implementing the ideas of Chanakya.

Employees

1

Safety and Security

THE DAYS OF CONVENTIONAL WARS, when kingdoms or nations fought with weapons like swords and later with sophisticated and more disastrous mass destruction weapons, are over. Now, wars are being fought between democracies with terrorism. The nature of these wars is more complex. This is the time when the importance of security cannot be undermined.

Terrorists target common people, the battlefields are public places and their aim is to disrupt economies. Corporate setups are soft targets and the only weapon we have is vigilance to prevent problems and the knowledge to fight back unanticipated disasters.

Chanakya says,

"For the guard not reporting to the city-superintendent an offence committed during the night whether by the animate or the inanimate, the punishment shall be in conformity with the offence, also in case of negligence." (2.36.42)

This means, an alert security person should be very alert. He has to report to his superiors every single offence that has been committed. He cannot take any seen or unseen movements for granted. If his superior also does not do this, even he shall be punished.

A special focus has to be given to corporate security personnel in the following manner:

- Extra Training

The guards, watchmen, and other security guards in your organisation have to be given extra training and information about the current scenario. They should be briefed about the threats faced by the country and the region specifically. You can also take the help of the local police, or intelligence agencies, to give them the latest updates about security measures suggested by the local, state, and union government.

- Support the Security Guards

All employees have to be made aware of the alarming situation we are in. They should cooperate with security officials. Being frisked and having your bags and personal belongings checked should not be taken as an act calculated to offend you. Do not feel insulted or ashamed. The security personnel is performing his duty. Be part of the system and help the system protect us.

- Work As a Team

It is important to note that it is not the duty of only the security guards to ensure security. Each employee has to play his/her role. Even security guards are human beings working round the clock to ensure safety. Understand their problems as well. Note that we have to work as a team.

Today, the nation, its economy, corporate houses, and our lives are under threat. And we have to rise and fight.

2

Selecting the Right Managers

AN EXECUTIVE MANAGER plays a key role in the successful functioning of a company. His selection and appointment is very important for the growth of the organisation. Headhunters and placement agencies provide resources and services for hiring the right candidate. However, the parameters have to be set by the employer.

Kautilya, in his *Arthashastra,* gives us detailed guidelines to follow while selecting managers who are fresh management trainees, and also those who are experienced and need to be directly recruited for higher responsibilities.

A. Selection of Management Trainees:

Book one, Chapter five, points out the various qualities that must be tested by the Human Resource department when it hunts for management trainees during campus interviews.

Kautilya says that a 'trainable' person is one who has the following six qualities:

1. Desire to Learn: Should be open-minded. After learning all the theories of management, a trainee should be eager to learn the practical side of it from seniors.
2. Effective Listening Ability: Listening is hearing plus thinking. He should be able to understand what is expected from him.

3. Ability to Reflect: He should be able to analyse a situation from various perspectives. Both logical and creative thinking is required in the field of management.
4. Ability to Reject False Views: He should be able to reach his own conclusions. He should be able to understand various points of view.
5. Intent on Truth, Not on Person: This is the ability to separate the person from the problem. He should be able to stick to the 'truth' that he has reached after his own careful analysis.

B. Selection of Experienced Managers

The qualities that must be tested before recruiting a person from another organisation is given in Book one, Chapter nine of the *Arthashastra.*

1. Technical Competence: This must be tested with the help of those people more learned in that science.
2. Intelligence, Perseverance, and Dexterity: His experience should also be coupled with the intelligence to understand the 'crux' of any problem. He should also have the ability to progress inspite of various hindrances.
3. Eloquence, Boldness, and Presence of Mind: He must have the ability to make quick decisions and a personality that reflects confidence. Eloquence also means to communicate words in a brief, yet effective manner.
4. Ability to Bear Troubles During Emergencies: The true test of a good manager comes during a crisis. He should be able to shoulder all responsibilities and execute an immediate action plan.

5. Uprightness, Friendliness, and Firmness of Devotion While Dealing With Others: He should be a people's man. Management is the ability to get the work done from the right people.
6. Strength of Character: Moral strength and ethical dealings have to be conveyed by action rather than just words.

3

Deciding Rank

DEGREES AND CERTIFICATES can never guarantee the results a manager can produce. Some of the best managers never completed their formal education. Neither Bill Gates, nor Henry Ford, needed an MBA before starting their respective companies.

A CEO has to focus on the results a person can bring about while recruiting his team of managers, not only their qualifications.

Kautilya says,

"From the capacity for doing work is the ability of the person judged. And in accordance with the ability, by suitably distributing rank among ministers and assigning place time and work to them he should appoint all the ministers." (1.8.28-29)

While the job responsibilities are being delegated to team members, Kautilya outlines five focus areas for a CEO.

• Capacity

The capacity for doing work is the key factor in

understanding a person's ability. Only an able person can bring out the best results. In many organisations, managers are recruited based on influence. However, if the person is not capable, the professionalism of the company suffers. One may get the 'chair' based on influence but the 'chair' will not let you be there for long.

- Rank/Designation

Rank and designation should be given based on the candidate's ability. In the current corporate world, we find that ranks are distributed freely. Even freshers are given senior positions without examining their output. The distribution of designations should be done based on the results produced. This is the key to success, particularly for many family-managed businesses in India.

- Place

A person needs to be appointed at the right place. In most industries, if a new branch is being opened, a preference is given to the local candidate. This is because he will understand more about that particular region than others. In the tourism industry every traveller prefers a local guide to an outsider, as locals know more details.

- Time

Timing has to be assigned to the person. First, the time by when he must join the project. Then, the timeframe has to be agreed upon to finish the project. Time-bound targets have to be set in order to bring out the best in a person.

- Work

The work expected to be done by that particular manager has to be defined. Management By Objectives (MBO), a concept of Key Result Area (KRA) gives a definite focus to the manager. This should be followed by a proper and regular feedback system.

When the above areas have been taken into account, it saves a lot of future misunderstanding and complications. Clear communication and an agreement to achieve the defined results not only makes a person effective, but also makes the organisation productive.

4

Stopping Attrition

THE BIGGEST CHALLENGE faced by any company is that of attrition, i.e. when employees leave the organisation.

Tackling this is the most important task of any and every HR department. Strategies and policies are eternally formulated to solve this problem. After all, continuous training, promotions and hikes in salaries are not enough to stem attrition.

Kautilya suggests,

"He should favour those contented, with additional wealth and honour. He should propitiate with gifts and conciliation those, who are discontented, in order to make them contented." (1.13.16-17)

There are generally two types of employees — content and discontented. Kautilya gives us a tip about handling these two types.

According to him, ignoring the employees who seem content (those who do not ask for a promotion, or a pay rise) is a very bad HR strategy. Every person works in the organisation for his salary. Just because the employee seems content does not mean that he/ she really is.

Such people just need a bigger offer from a competitor, and they will be gone like the wind. Hence, if you see a content employee, favour him with additional wealth, awards, and also increments. You will find that they will be more loyal to you. Why? Well, you understood their needs even before they expressed their feelings. After this, there would be no unions or strikes!

As for those who are very restless and discontent, give gifts and other notable benefits to them as well to retain them in the organisation.

There are a few more useful tips that can be followed to avoid attrition.

- Give Importance to HRD (Human Resource Department)

Most top managements consider the HR department to be very ordinary and merely the administrative part of their organisation. Its function is only to recruit, train employees, and maintain their records. In fact, each and every manager should consider the HR to be the top priority in their agenda. Work on your people. Only then will your people work for you.

- CEO Should Be a Mentor

A CEO should be a friend, philosopher and guide to all the employees. Running the business is only a small part of his job. His main job is to be a teacher and train people to become future leaders. He should use his years of experience in running a business to train others to do the same.

- Create Your Own Culture

Instead of copying from others, develop your own culture — an organisational culture that is unique. Others can copy your product and services, but never your culture. Such a culture should be friendly and open. Every employee should feel that he is part of a family.

Break all the rules. Get out of your cabin and spend more time with your staff. Let your organisition be the one where every one feels proud to work.

5

Changing Jobs

LET'S FACE IT. There comes a point in each and every person's career when he feels like running away from his routine, almost mundane, job. He feels like taking up a higher responsibility and earning more than what he is currently getting.

For such people Kautilya advises,

"One who is conversant with the ways of the world, should seek service with a king, endowed with personal excellences and the excellences of material constituents, through such as dear and beneficial (to the king)." (5.4.1)

Such an experienced person, who is equipped with the know-how of his work, should definitely seek higher responsibilities. If not, he will feel depressed, stressed, and underutilised.

He should approach the king (leaders of organisations)

and after recounting or presenting a summary of his experience and results achieved in the past, should ask for a better job. Now, changing jobs does not mean changing organisations. You can change jobs even within the organisation.

However, while doing so, one should keep in mind the benefits that he can bring to the owner, not just to himself. It is very important to remember that while one is being interviewed for higher positions/responsibilities, the interviewer will always consider the benefits the recruiting firm can get. Hence, keep that foremost in mind.

Steps that will help you take up higher responsibilities:

- Gather Experience

Experience counts a lot when it comes to going up in life. Learn from everyone and everything possible. Update your knowledge and gather some good skills. The more experienced you are, the better your chances of going up in life.

- Prepare a Document

While approaching the people who could promote you, or give you new responsibilities, always carry documents which show your successful endeavours. CVs, portfolios, certificates, press cuttings, reports of the projects you have handled — all these could be helpful.

- Talk about 'Their' Benefits

During the interview, it is very important to discuss the benefits that you can give to your organisation. Talk in terms of definite numbers. Do a little bit of research as you prepare for the interview.

Whatever new assignment you take up, you have to leave your mark.

Bob Dole, a former American leader who ran for the US Presidency, once said, "When it's all over, it's not who you were. It's whether you made a difference."

6

The First Step

MOST OF US WAIT for the right opportunity to start looking for our dream job. We wait for a 'wanted' advertisement to appear in the newspaper before even thinking of making the next jump in our career. Even businessmen wait for information to get the 'dream' contract.

This is a big mistake!

Even if our dream job or project is currently not available in the market, we can create the opportunity. Chanakya was a great believer in making efforts ourselves rather than depending on fate or destiny to shape up situations. He says,

"One trusting in fate, being devoid of human endeavour, perishes, because he does not start undertakings, or his undertakings have miscarried (failed)." (7.11.34)

Obviously, if opportunities don't knock on our doors, we go to the opportunities and knock on their doors! Now how does one do that?

Here are a few tips:

- Know Your Strengths

Before you go around banging on doors, do a little bit of introspection. Know your strengths. Focus on what you are good at. Chanakya calls this a person's '*Swadharma*' (what one is naturally capable of doing). Create your dream work/project to which you can deliver better than others. Prepare your résumé or business plan, clearly highlighting your past experience and what makes you different from the others.

- Tap the Right Persons

A good résumé or business plan is not enough in itself. We have to market ourselves. For this, it is important to know who the right people are and which companies would like to use our services. Mail your proposal, call up, and ask for an appointment. Finally, turn up on time and have a word with the right people. A face-to-face meeting is an absolute must. Don't wait for someone to call you. There are many companies that have vacancies and projects to be executed, but do not advertise.

- Be Clear about the Financials

Let's be honest, there are no free lunches. Before you pitch yourself, also think about how much money you want to make from this new initiative. During meetings, you must speak and work on the financials and economics involved. A win-win situation can happen only when our roles, goals, and more importantly, the financials are clear.

Remember that when you finally get your dream job or project, it is not enough. In fact, it's just the beginning. Then you must deliver what you have promised.

Show your capability, not just by words but by result-oriented actions too. And learn to work with others, for that's the secret for succeeding in any project.

7

Death on Duty

LIFE IS VERY PRECIOUS and the death of a person brings great sorrow to his near and dear ones. However, if he dies while he is on duty, then the death also becomes the responsibility of the employer.

Despite the best safety measures and policies made to avoid accidents, there is a possibility that an employee may lose his life during work.

Kautilya's advice for such unforeseen circumstances is:

"Of those dying while on duty, the sons and wives shall receive the food and wages. And their minor children, old and sick persons should be helped. And he should grant them money and do honour on occasions of death, illness, and birth ceremonials." (5.3.28-30)

For organisations like the defence forces, the government has worked out the compensation in such cases. But, what needs to be noted here is that Kautilya wants the employer to not just give the family financial compensation but, in fact, take on bigger responsibilities.

He suggests that the employer should consider the family of the deceased employee as his own family.

He should not only look after their basic needs like food and financial assistance but also consider the needs of the children like education, mentoring, and guidance. 'Honour on occasions' — to use the exact words.

Once an accident took place in a highly respected Indian company, and 60 employees lost their lives. The media asked the head of the corporate giant, "How much money are you planning to give their families?"

His answer was typical of the company's employer-friendly policies, "It will depend on each family's need."

Unlike our politicians, who announce a fixed sum of compensation for all families, the top company official had decided to understand the need of each family.

If some family required more money, it was given. Similarly, if someone required assistance in rehabilitation, it was provided, if a child needed education, it was taken care of. That approach shows concern.

Here are some tips for facing such situations in today's scenario:

- Insurance

Make sure that each of your employees has a life insurance. Have your HR department ensure that each employee has at least one policy in effect.

- Understand Each Employee

Each person in your organisation has different family needs. Keep a record of their family members — how many people in the family, what they do, and so on. Organise family meets to ensure a good family-worklife balance.

- Be There

When an employee loses his life, meet the family. Do not

just send a manager with a cheque. Be present with the family and share their pain.

As someone has said beautifully, "After the death of a near one, I often wished for a few words of love, rather than the tears of thousands of people."

8

Taking Care of Employees

NOW THIS IS MORE for your boss than you! Still, read on, as the ever-booming economy may someday help you establish a business and employ people yourself. And when you do that, you will soon realise that good, talented, and skilled people are really rare.

Ask anyone in the HR department. Not only do they have to recruit and train people, but they have to also retain people within the organisation. In the end, it must be realised that it is not the brand nor even the salary that can retain people — it's the human touch the organisation is capable of giving.

For this, Chanakya suggests that the management needs to be totally aware of what the employees think — if they don't, they are playing with danger,

"Not being rooted among the subjects, he becomes easy to uproot." (8.2.18)

Here are a few steps to do this:

- Take Time Out for Your Employees

It is important to spend time with all your subordinates,

individually. There is just no substitute for this. Set aside half an hour every day for this purpose. This will help you understand the way each employee thinks and can help resolve problems as they first start to appear.

- Get Out of Your Cabin

Do not sit in your cabin and give orders over the phone. Now and then, get out of our cabin and walk to the employees' desk and work stations. There are many benefits in doing this — one, this acts as a surprise check. Secondly, you will directly know what is happening in the office.

- Plan an Outing

There are limits in an office. An outing with your team, a celebration of major events at a different venue, a party or picnic, will not only reduce the stress levels but also help everyone emotionally relate to each other. Many talents are discovered during informal celebrations and gatherings.

- Keep Records

Now, this is the most important part. Maintain a different file for each employee with the help of the HR department. It should document the details of each employee. Record keeping is not enough; the management should look at it from time to time and make effective use of the employees by looking up their inherent strengths.

A recent survey to find out the best employer among the corporates indicated that employees who feel 'wanted and challenged' in a work place have better chances of staying committed to the company for a longer period of time.

This is better reflected in what the American industrialist Charles Erwin Wilson once said, "A good boss makes his men realise they have more ability than they think they have, so that they consistently do better work than they thought they could."

9

Security Above Salary

I HAVE ONCE AGAIN decided to deal with the topic of attrition. Many are still surprised at the gigantic proportions this problem has taken. ALL the organisations face attrition today. Consultants are being appointed, research is being conducted and new methods and strategies are being sought out to understand why people leave organisations!

The first reason that people think of is that employees leave due to higher salaries offered by other companies. However, it is clearly seen that money or higher salaries alone cannot reduce the attrition rate.

Chanakya gives us food for thought,

"Even for a very large sum of money, no one would desire the loss of his life." (8.3.35)

So what is it that makes people shift jobs, or change companies? The answer is multifold.

- The Immediate Boss

There is a popular saying, 'People don't leave companies, they leave their bosses!' Your immediate boss is a reflection of the whole organisation. The Chairman may be the best leader in the industry, but he may not be able to reach the last man in the organisation. The heads of department, the middle managers, the line managers, all of them become a source of inspiration for the people working immediately below them. If this person is a good leader, people will be inspired to work. If he is not, even those in blue chip companies will quit their jobs.

- Salary

Yes, this is important. You cannot keep your employees dedicated and faithful to the company on an empty stomach. People need to earn good money and also receive a hike once in a while. Note that the 'high' salary an employee demands is not automatically the 'right' salary. The environment also plays a major role in the expenses of the individual. The cost of living in a particular place, the number of people who are dependent on his income, his lifestyle — all have an impact on determining the salary expectations of the individual.

- Security

This factor is the topmost on any employee's mind. How does one define security? It has many aspects. Financial security, mental security, and also a feeling of being at the right place at the right time. The definition of security will also change from person to person and even from generation to generation.

I was conversing with a top management professional from a multinational company who has spent over 25 years in the same firm, despite better offers. When I tried to find out why, he explained, "Ours is a human company. More than the salary, it was the fact that we always felt at home." Try to achieve this 'family-feeling' in your organisation.

10

Command Promotion

GETTING PROMOTED SHOULD not be demanded, it should be commanded. Promotion from one position to the next is directly related to the results produced.

Regarding promotions, Chanakya tells the leaders,

"He (king) should make those his ministers who, when appointed to tasks, the income from which is calculated (beforehand), would bring in the income as directed or more, since (thus) their qualities are proved." (1.8.13)

The quality of a person is proved by his output. But here, Kautilya becomes more specific emphasising the productivity of the employee by saying that promotion is to be considered according to the income the employee brings to the organisation. Such a person should be made a minister (at a senior managerial position).

During a job interview, the employer talks about the pay package in terms of CTC (Cost to Company). At this point in time, the employer calculates the expenses he would incur for the candidate, if he were to recruit him. The employer will also look into the probable revenue generated by the candidate and accordingly, decide upon the package.

If given a particular assignment or project, the manager has a fixed budget within which he has to operate. There is also a particular profit expected from the project. If at the end of the project the expected profits (or more profits) are made, or even budgeted expenses are reduced, such a person should be considered for promotion.

So what can an employee learn from the above *sutra*?

- Make a Financial Contribution

Every employee irrespective of the department he belongs to should make a financial contribution justifying the remuneration paid by his organisation.

Dr Makrand Tare, an Human Resource Management (HRD) specialist was addressing a group of HR managers. He said, "Even if you are in HR, you should contribute to your company in terms of financial gains, either by bringing down costs or by increasing the productivity of your employees."

- Show Your Result in Numbers

Just because you have made a financial contribution, do not just sit back. Show your results to your seniors by presenting them with numbers. Make a report, make a graph and tell your bosses how you, being a part of the project, have made a significant contribution. Learn to sell yourself at every stage of your career.

- Think Like an Employer

Give more than you take. Do not expect a promotion or an increment at the end of each year. Ask yourself, what your boss wants from you. Work in that direction. Produce more wealth for your organisation than what you consume.

An MBA student during his campus interview was asked, "What is your salary expectation?" His answer was, "Sir, that is for you to decide at this stage. At the end of six months let us review my performance. Then I will tell you what my expectation is." He was immediately recruited.

11

Make People Accountable

WHILE IT'S DIFFICULT TO get the right people for the right job, it's even more difficult to make the people currently working with you be productive and efficient.

Chanakya has a solution for this — if employees are not productive, then impose a fine on them!

Chanakya provides an example:

"He (the leader) should wait for one month, if the (accounts officer) has not brought in the day-to-day accounts, after one month, the (officer) shall pay a fine of two hundred panas increased (by that amount) for each succeeding month." (2.7.26)

However, this system is to be implemented one step at a time, according to Chanakya who lists the tactics called *Sama*, *Dana*, *Bheda*, and *Danda*.

But how do we follow this system? Here are some tips:

- Define What Is Expected

This is the first step. Clearly spell out what is expected from the employee. Most problems start when we do not communicate our expectations clearly. A well-defined job profile and job description will help a person understand his role. One way of doing this is to document these roles and expectations. The best way is to make the person himself write it, lest he forgets.

- Regular Supervision

Keep an eye on the person who is doing the work. Regular supervision, and asking the right questions will help if the employee is about to lose direction. This does not mean that you need to be 'bossy' or restrict a person. You must allow the employee freedom to carry out the task in his or her style. You need not define 'how' but you will have to define 'what' and 'why'. It's important that the person maintains his focus on his productivity.

- Reminders and Following-Up

When you do this for the first time, it will take some time for the person to understand. However, with patience and practice, incorporate this into a system which runs the show, rather than doing this yourself! Of course, if you keep issuing reminders and the work still doesn't get done, then it is time to take some serious action.

- The Fine

Chanakya suggested that the unproductive employee must be fined! Just announcing this, or making this part of the company policy will not help. One has to implement it from time to time. This will get rid of lethargy and the employee will act quickly to protect himself. It will also send out the message that you are serious about your business and no one can take his work for granted.

If each person in an organisation works with optimum productivity as per the goals defined, the business world itself would be different!

12

Safety in Any Deal-Making

IN ANY LEADER'S LIFE, there comes a moment when he has to take some critical decisions while striking a big deal. At times, he has to consider the deal's financial impact, the impact on the morale (of the employees) and also any future impact it may have on the market position he currently holds.

During such difficult times, when he has do decide between the present and the future, Chanakya suggests that the leader consider the safety angle first.

Chanakya says,

"He should not follow that policy by resorting to which he were to see the ruin of his own undertakings, not of (those of) the other party." *(7.1.24)*

So, while going in for that big deal, always consider these aspects:

- The Financial Aspect

Business is about wealth creation, wealth management and wealth expansion. As a leader, one should not ignore this critical angle. Secure the wealth that you have created, manage the existing wealth and focus on the wealth that can be created in the future. Be non-emotional while dealing with this aspect. However, emotions cannot be left out all the time. This is where the next aspect comes in...

- The Human Aspect

The key asset in any organisation is the human one — those who created it, and run it. You not only have to take care of their well-being and development, you also have to consider the impact on their morale.

A huge team without any enthusiasm is nothing when compared to a smaller group with an 'enthusiastic' drive to change and excel. It's this enthusiasm which makes the difference in a war.

- The Social Aspect

This is very important. Even if the previous two aspects are taken care of while concluding a deal, never miss out on the social impact it may have. The deal may make a lot of money for the employees and also the shareholders, but if it causes problems in the environment, ecology, or nature, you need to think twice about the deal.

In the movie *Sarkar*, which was inspired by *The Godfather*, there is a similar negotiation scene. A drug-dealer comes to the Don and offers him a big deal for getting the necessary sanctions for a drug-shipment meant for the new-found market.

The money offered for clearing the consignment was huge, but the Don refused it since he found that even if he or his team made the money, it would cause a great problem for youngsters and the future generations.

It's not easy, but it's important to negotiate. The 'thought' that is put into the deal-making process, the 'study' and research all have an impact on the final outcome.

So sharpen your intellect, broaden your heart and, with maturity, strike the deal.

13

Welcoming Back Ex-Workers

CHANGING JOBS FREQUENTLY is a very common occurrence in today's corporate world. Gone are the days when a person retired from the same organisation which gave him his first salary cheque.

The reasons why people quit are many, but the most important reason is that they do not find growth possibilities, or that their immediate boss is not effective enough to retain or inspire them further.

But, there is one more scenario. What if someone who quit the organisation wants to come back? Now this is a dilemma for the decision-maker.

Chanakya guides us on what to do:

"One deserting because of the master's fault and returning because of his virtue, (or) deserting because of the enemy's virtue and returning because of his fault, is one deserting and returning on good grounds, fit to be made peace with." (7.6.24)

So you need to get a complete perspective — Why did the person quit? Why has this person come back? And what are the benefits or loss that it can lead to?

Let's look at these parameters in detail:

- Why Did the Person Quit?

Be honest — was it your fault as a leader that he left? In that case, he is worthy of returning if you have learnt your lesson and are already working on improving your leadership skills.

Was it in a fit of anger that you fired the person? Or was it some miscommunication? Did the person quit because he found something good in the new employer? In that case also, it is a fault with the leadership, because you did not have that 'quality' which your competitor has.

In both cases, the person should be welcomed back.

- Was the Person Right?

There are issues and situations that were not under the control of the person quitting. For example, at that time, he required a pay scale (as a necessity) which you could not provide.

Or, did the person realise that it was his mistake to quit as your organisation was really better and genuinely wants to come back and work productively? In this case too he could be welcomed back.

- The Person's Virtues

The final check point! What is the value-addition the person brings? Probably, the person has a skill or art that only he possesses, and is already in demand in the industry as he is really 'good' at the work he does. Even in this case, the person can be welcomed back.

Whether you do all these calculations or not, it's finally your gut feeling that matters. You have to take a decision and look ahead. Looking back at the past is good, but moving ahead is more important.

14

Tackling Attrition

BIG BRANDS CAN ATTRACT employees, but they cannot retain them. A recent study revealed that it's the biggest brands that face the highest level of attrition. Surprisingly, smaller companies — some without a proper HR department — enjoy a near-zero attrition rate. Now, this is worthy of research.

In larger organisations, work is totally dependent on key people. Yet, as stated above, there is no guarantee that they will stay in the company forever. Now, how can one ensure that the required work is done despite attrition?

Chanakya suggests:

"He should establish (each) department with many heads and without permanency (of tenure of office)." (2.9.31)

People may run organisations. However, good organisations are run by good systems along with good people.

Therefore, one of the strategies that Chanakya suggests is to make a system that takes attrition into account right from day one.

In the above verse, he suggests some key strategic points for the job-profiling of senior people:

- 'Many Heads'

The head of any particular project or department is a key person. The dependency of an organisation on this person is very high. Chanakya suggests reversing this dependency — split the responsibility.

When he uses the phrase 'many heads' he means that if you require one head, have three heads instead. The reason? If one person leaves, there are still two more to look after things. The work continues without a break as the others take over.

So prepare all three heads with equal training and trust.

A company once had a vacancy for a President's post. But it appointed three Vice-Presidents instead and split the job. Amazing results were achieved. In the long run, they ended up with two highly productive Presidents.

- 'Without Permanency'

No one is permanent in this world, including the founder himself. What remains permanent are the vision and the goodwill created because of the work one has done. Therefore, with people too, do not expect permanency.

When you work with this attitude, you will give your best. The best way to make yourself permanent is to make more duplicates like you. Even if one duplicate is close to what you are, you have done your job. Let them take over and continue from where you have stopped.

- 'Establish'

The only way of ensuring non-dependency on people is continuous training. Now this is not just a formal process, rather, it's the very 'lifeline' of any organisation, the very breath that keeps it alive.

If we study organisations that have lasted for generations, we will find that they have put in place good systems along with continuous training. Adapt these and see the positive changes that it will lead to.

15

Quality Control

THERE ARE TWO KINDS OF players in any sector — those who offer high quality at a high price, and those who offer low quality for a low price. A customer chooses between the two depending on his priority.

However, no one can compromise on quality when it comes to critical items like food, beverages, and medicines. Otherwise, it could prove fatal for the consumer.

Chanakya not only emphasised the importance of quality checks, but also set up government control methods in his day to ensure that quality of products did not suffer.

"For perishable goods, a retraction may be allowed with the restriction: 'It shall not be sold elsewhere'. In case of transgression of that, the fine is twenty-four panas or one-tenth of the goods." (3.15.7-8)

In the above verse, we see that only for perishable commodities Chanakya sets a policy that it has to be consumed within a particular region. He even defines the punishment if this is not followed.

How does one ensure high quality products and services in one's own organisation? Here are some tips:

- Understand the Meaning of Quality

The meaning of quality changes from person to person and also from market to market. It differs completely from one segment to another. For example, a person who always used to wear torn clothes will consider even a second-hand but decent shirt as 'high quality'.

A person who is privileged to wear clean and good clothes will consider only a branded shirt or designer wear to be 'high quality'. So understand this mindset and your customer's requirements to define what quality means. Another example would be the exporters who send second-hand Indian clothes to poorer nations as against the domestic textile industry.

- Set Up Parameters

It is important to set up parameters to ensure quality before sending, or marketing, the produced goods and services. All well-known brands have quality control departments which monitor processes in their factories at each and every level, rather than just at the final stage.

No wonder then that these departments are called quality 'assurance' instead of quality 'control'. Each person at every stage of production is therefore responsible for guaranteeing the quality.

- Improving Continuously

The demand in the market is growing, the needs of the customers are changing. Hence, the definition of quality also changes from time to time. Understand this and improve accordingly.

In a shrinking world, it's better to pitch ahead and make products that reach global standards. Therefore, it pays to apply concepts like Total Quality Management (TQM), ISO certifications, etc, in your processes and systems. Above all, learn from your mistakes, accept customer feedback and adopt the same in the next level of improvement of your quality standards.

16

Selecting the Right Person

NOW THIS IS A CHALLENGE THAT the HR departments face the most. But, today, almost every section chief has to take on the role of an HR person not only to keep his team intact, but to also strengthen it further.

That's because companies now fight more for people than for market share. Still, you can't recruit every other person. You have to carefully select the right candidates from all the applicants, and an interview is the most critical entry point as it determines the future of the new recruit as well as of the company.

Apart from salary, post, and job profile, Chanakya suggests that it is important to know the 'thinking', 'mind-set', and 'psychology' of the candidate:

"On finding out, he should keep him in accordance with his intentions." (7.6.29)

But which questions should one ask during interviews? Here are some examples:

- 'Who is Your Role Model?'

Interviews usually start with the interviewer asking, "Tell me something about yourself." The very next query should be, "Who is your role model?" This is a very different, yet powerful question.

The answer will tell you about the candidate's thinking pattern, because a role model is a person one usually thinks about, relates to, and even tries to copy.

If a person says Bill Gates, you will know that there is a businessman or an IT professional inside him who is seeking an opportunity. If it's Gandhiji or any spiritual guru, it means that the person values noble ideals and gives importance to 'ethics' in life.

- 'Whom Do You Spend Time With?'

It's important to know the interests and lifestyle of the person beyond office hours. If the answer is 'family', you know he is a family man.

If the person's free time is mostly spent in libraries or with friends, you know he is seeking education and knowledge, or just companionship, respectively.

As the old saying goes, "Company makes the man."

- 'Suppose You Were Asked To....?'

It would help to give the person a cultural shock by forecasting a change in job profile. For example, if you are interviewing a Chartered Accountant for a senior financial post, ask him, "What if we ask you to head the marketing department in a year's time?"

The answer will tell you his ability for 'change management'. The more a person is adaptable to change, the more the benefit for both the parties.

Make the interview fun and mentally challenging, rather than just a mundane recruitment process.

If you interview a job candidate in this manner, you will understand the human mind better, and even accurately predict if the candidate will have a successful career in your firm.

17

Don't Beat Around the Bush

DOES THIS SITUATION RING A BELL? You desperately want to discuss something important with your boss. When you finally work up the nerve to enter his cabin, you start off by talking about everything, except what you really want to tell him.

Slowly, you see your boss getting irritated. In a worst-case scenario, your boss screams, "Please come to the point…fast!" By then, he's surely prejudiced against you.

You have to understand that people who reach the top are inherently sharp and can understand the 'core issue' very quickly. So when you are with them, do not beat around the bush.

Now after understanding this point, look at the same situation from the point of view of the leader. Our seniors always like to work with people who are sharp and can understand things immediately.

Even Chanakya had some very practical advice for leaders when it comes to choosing their subordinates. He said,

"The demand is to be made only once, not twice." (5.2.30)

In other words, a leader should be surrounded by workers who need to be told anything just *once*. And if you ensure you are good enough to be part of this crack team, your career is made:

- Be Among the Right People

All great leaders invariably have great teams, which were formed by ensuring that the right people were selected.

Remember, we are talking not of the whole team but the core 'strategic' team. This will be the think-tank of the organisation. It requires mature, sharp, and brilliant people. If you work hard enough to get into this team, your most important work is done.

- Gain the Vision

Even though you may be sharp, you still need training to gain the same vision that your seniors have for the organisation. This has to be done in the right manner.

If you are really good, just one logical explanation with facts and figures will be enough. You and your team will then be a part of the senior's dream and the journey itself will be smooth.

- Stay in Touch

Hurdles are bound to exist and they come back in some form or the other. So you have to stay in touch with the leader as you need to make sure that you and your team are not drifting from the plan.

Keep yourself focused towards your objective and make sure that the entire team is doing this too.

Always remember that gaining leadership yourself is not just about strategies, but also about being part of a strategic team. Once your team is ready, any demand you make will surely be made only once, not twice.

18

Reward Productive People

ALL OF US ARE SURROUNDED by people who believe that it's just not worth making extra efforts at the job if the salary is fixed. This is where the theory of productivity and incentives kicks in — the more you work, the more rewards you will get.

But the onus is on the boss and the firm's owners to identify the productive people in their organisations and not only reward them, but also make them stay.

Chanakya had a strategy in place for this:

"In case more work is done than agreed upon, he shall not make the effort vain." (3.14.11)

In addition to this being a rule for paying out bonuses, the above verse can also be used as a yardstick to check if employees are good — just check if they have done far more than what they were expected to do.

If the answer is yes, then the management has to ensure that their 'extra' efforts are rewarded. But how can a boss keep track of his employees' productivity?

- Keep Notes

It's important that the director, CEO, or even the head of a department keep notes of people who are productive. People who are sincere, dedicated, and committed are essential in every company. Such people are the pillars of any organisation. While it's good to keep mental notes of the staff's performance, it would be best if these could be written down for future reference.

- Look for New Opportunities

A leader should keep looking not only for new business opportunities but also for opportunities that can be given to productive people. The basic thought should be that an employee who has been very productive and dedicated to the company needs to be part of any new and wonderful assignment which offers better rewards.

- Promote When Required

When seniors in an organisation find that certain people are good, they should not hesitate to promote them. Promotion means far more than just giving a higher designation. It can mean salary hikes, a share in profits, or even an opportunity to head a new venture. Thus, the person also feels empowered and recognised within the company.

They say, "People do not leave organisations, they leave their bosses." But, according to me, "People should not leave their organisations due to lack of identification of their skill by their bosses!"

19

Take the Initiative

A GOOD LEADER INSPIRES EVERY follower and makes him productive — be it community leaders, spiritual leaders, or corporate leaders. In the presence of the master, everyone feels safe and secure. But the real challenge is when the big boss is not around.

There are two situations which may force a boss to not come in to work. Either it was planned and others were informed about his or her absence, or the boss has to deal with some emergency.

In either case, the subordinates are supposed to take charge. Chanakya says:

"The minister should take steps in case of calamity of the king." (5.6.1)

So, if the king is not around, the minister should take charge. If the Director or CEO is not present, the managers — or if the boss is not around, the subordinates — should take charge.

But, how does one go about this?

- Observe the Boss

So many of us follow a leader, yet forget to understand the leader. Following the leader is good, but understanding the leader is much more important. This is a skill that every person has to develop.

Whenever you are around the boss, observe him. Ask yourself, why does he do this? What does he really want?

Try to read between the lines and listen to the unsaid words. As the great Jesuit priest and psychotherapist Anthony de Mello said, "The words of a master seem ordinary, but have foreign meaning."

- Start Taking Small Decisions

Good leaders expect their team to take the right decisions in the overall interest of the company or country. However, if you do not have this habit, start taking small decisions yourself even when the boss is around. Taking small decisions will give you the confidence needed to take big decisions.

- Take Charge

Finally, when the boss is not around, the followers have to take charge. There should not be a vacuum just because the leader is absent. The show must go on. Each person should think like the boss and be a good boss himself.

Once, the leader of a successful organisation was asked how the company managed to maintain its good performance even after the Founder had passed away. He replied, "The master is gone, but he left behind masterpieces!"

20

Want to Be a Good Boss?

SURVEYS HAVE REPEATEDLY PROVED that one of the biggest reasons why people leave an organisation is because they cannot work under their boss. To be an ideal leader, or a good boss, is an eternal challenge.

A good boss is not produced in B-schools, nor with the help of management lectures and seminars.

But Chanakya gives us a hint:

"And, in all cases, he should favour the stricken (subjects) like a father." (4.3.43)

In our own homes, the role of a father has been well-defined. He is full of love and concern. At the same time, he is also a strict disciplinarian. But whatever the case, a father will never abandon his children.

Here are some tips for you to adopt with your subordinates to become a good boss:

- Understand Them

Always remember that an employee is not just a money-generating machine. They have a life outside the office. They have a family, a friend circle, and also various interests and hobbies. It is important to understand their total personality. Once you understand their expectations, it will be easy to manage those expectations. Only then will you be able to tune into your employees.

- Give Time to Educate Them

No good parent will ever expect the child to work and make money for them from Day One. Similarly, your employees have to be educated, instructed, and prepared before they meet bigger challenges. Even you have to be part of their training and development. No doubt they will make mistakes and just like children fall when they try to walk, so will employees stumble in the course of their duty. But with support and self confidence, they will one day run faster than you.

- Discipline with Love

The greatest challenge for any parent is to know the balance between discipline and love. The solution is love with discipline and discipline with love. An area has to be demarcated — a framework has to indicated — beyond which there is dangerous territory. Subordinates, like children, are full of energy and enthusiasm. It is important to encourage their creativity. But it is equally important to give direction to their work. Discipline, coupled with love, is the answer.

Finally, whatever you do, remember that no classroom lectures can achieve what one learns from direct experience. Therefore, in your own maturity, understand that in spite of your best efforts, the employee may still make the same mistakes that you did. Accept it with love and grace.

There is a beautiful phrase I am reminded of, "A man learns that his father was right, when his son tells him that he is wrong!" Maybe we will need to remember this while dealing with our employees.

Finance

21

Net Profit Counts!

I ONCE MET A SUCCESSFUL French businessman who had started his business from scratch. It was while he was sharing his success stories with me that I got an insight into how beginners in the business field misunderstand 'profits'.

He said, "First-level businessmen always feel income is profit. Once they mature in running a business, they realise that real profit is what comes after calculating the expenses and taxes."

Now, this French businessman was merely echoing words that were first written by Chanakya two thousand years ago,

"When assigned work, he should show income cleared of expenses." (5.5.1)

This is a simple, yet most important basic, lesson for the head of a business unit or profit centre. Such people, when they report to their head or board of directors, always show numbers, which is the top line (incoming). Now it's nice to have a good turnover, but sales are *not* profits.

But how do we understand this difference? Let us take it step-by-step:

- Top-line

The sales numbers (what is sold and orders that have been confirmed) is generally called the 'Top-Line'. These numbers are what people look at. "We reached a 100 crore figure this year." This statement would generally mean that the sales that particular year have touched a figure of 100 crore. Sales are the revenue for any organisation. It is also called 'ITB' (In The Box), the sales pipeline that have been converted into confirmed orders.

- Expenses

Sales bring money into an organisation. This incoming is the cash flow of the organisation. A regular and strong cash flow is the backbone of any business. After this, expenses take place. Salaries to the staff, investment in infrastructure like office, technology, and information systems are calculated. Next, we have other overheads like travel, marketing cost, training etc. All this put together are the total expenses of the company. As the company grows its top-line, its expenses also grow accordingly.

- Bottom Line

What is left from sales minus the expenses are your profits — the Bottom line. This is what differentiates successful businesses from sick businesses. There are companies that have great top lines but small bottom lines. Yes, now there are other factors as well — like taxes, total assets and their valuation etc. However, what the shareholders will generally look at is the dividend which is now called the real bottom line.

Adi Godrej, Chairman of the Godrej group of companies had summarised it briefly, "Sales is Vanity, Profit is Sanity, Cash is Reality!" Understand this basic principle and you will understand how to make your company more profitable.

22

Take Care of the Treasury in Difficult Times

THE KING (LEADER) PLAYS a very important role in any organisation. He has to take care of all his subjects (employees). The only way to do this is if the king has financial stability and security. So, keeping his treasury full should be the leader's prime concern.

Therefore, Chanakya advises us:

"The (king) without a treasury should collect a treasury, when difficulties concerning money have arisen." (5.2.1)

There will always be difficult times, when money does not come into a treasury. Even during these times, a king has to carry on with collecting revenues and keep the business going.

This is a major challenge for any organisation's leader. But the following tips will help make the organisation financially stable:

- Budget

Money may keep flowing into an organisation, but it also goes out at double the speed it comes in! Controlling this outflow is possible only if one plans in advance. You should have a system similar to the dam on a river which helps in storing water so that it can be used as per our convenience.

- Learn about Finance

One very important aspect of financial management is to

continuously learn financial skills. As your company grows, the financial challenges grow too.

It starts from the capital requirement stage, and then comes the short-term 'running capital' requirement, and, if not tracked well, there could even be a debt-stage which can prove fatal for the organisation. So, keep learning new financial skills about investments, tax structuring, etc.

- Network

This suggestion may not seem to be related to financial planning, but it is very important. It's our friend circle and the network of goodwill that we have created which will help us during financial crises.

Yes, in spite of all our planning, there are times when things can go terribly wrong. Then how will you fill up your treasury? It will be this network which will prove helpful at that time.

Be proactive in creating a good friend circle. As they say, "The best time to make friends is before you need them." Friends make you richer not only in monetary terms but also in the help you get while facing challenges in life.

As Swami Chinmayanandaji said, "To have a friend, you need to be a friend first."

23

Wages

FOR CHANAKYA, THE SUBJECTS and their welfare was more important than kingship. Every idea in the *Arthashastra* is directed towards this end. Thus every CEO has to take into consideration the welfare of his employees first, which will ultimately benefit him. The *Arthashastra* clearly shows that Kautilya envisioned the welfare of society,

"In the happiness of the subjects lies the benefit of the king and in what is beneficial to the subjects is his own benefit." (1.19.34)

Arthashastra evolved a wage structure, which provides the protection of workers against exploitation, or unduly low wages, and also facilitated justice and fairness for the sound relationship between the employer and the employee.

- Consideration for Employees

What had been visualised by Kautilya in 4 B.C. found its way in the Minimum Wages Act of 1948. It recognises that wages cannot be determined by market forces of supply and demand alone. Workers also were allowed to choose their work and enter into a contract before starting any work.

If the employee gets sick he is also given due consideration,

"If he is incapable due to ill health or due to a calamity, he shall get an extension." (3.14.2)

Whatever salary was fixed for labourers, the master was obliged to pay it, and in case the rule was violated, he had to undergo punishment,

"In case of non-payment of the wage, the fine is twelve panas or five times the wage." (3.13.34)

- Consideration of the Employers

However, the wage structure was not one-sided. The employer's efforts were also safeguarded. Productivity of the workers was taken into consideration while paying wages,

"A wage is for work done, not for what is not done." (3.14.8)

According to Kautilya, if the labourer after receiving the wages, did not complete his work he was fined,

"An employee not doing the work after receiving the wage, the fine is twelve panas, and detention till it is done." (3.14.1)

If the employee did not return to his work, the master was at liberty to engage another worker,

"In case the employee misses the time (or completion) or does the work in a wrong manner, he may complete the work through another." (3.14.10-14)

- Deciding a Fair Wage

But how do we decide what is the correct wage? For this, we will have to meet the current industry standards and also consider the time and effort that is put in a job,

"The payment of the wages was decided on the basis of work done, time spent in doing it, at the rate prevailing at the time." (3.13.27)

This concept has been adopted by the committee of Fair Wages, Government of India, set up in 1949 which prescribed,

"The prevailing rates of wages in the same or similar occupations in the same or neighbouring localities." (Report of the Committee of Fair Wages, Delhi, 1954).

24

Budgeting

THE TERM 'BUDGET' SIGNIFIES estimation and organisation of revenue and expenditure of an organisation or state. A strong financial foundation is necessary for an organisation or state to be sound and stable. Good budgeting is the basis of a strong financial architecture. Hence, financial management plays a prominent role in the development of any organisation or country.

"All undertakings are dependent first on the treasury. Therefore, he (the leader) should look to the treasury first." (2.8.1)

The CEO of an organisation is advised to focus on increasing the revenue and cash flow into the treasury. He is also recommended a good management system to take care of budgeting. Forecasting the details of financial management constitute the exercise of budgeting.

Kautilya emphasises that the officer-in-charge of finance (the CFO in today's corporate world) should concentrate all his efforts on increasing income and reducing expenditure.

The details of each financial activity, including record keeping, types of income and control of expenditure and taxation is given in Book two, Chapter seven of *Arthashastra.*

• Accounting Systems

"He (leader) should check the accounts for each day, group of five days, fortnight, month, four months and a year." (2.7.30)

The leader is expected to maintain a system of daily,

weekly, monthly, and yearly accounting systems to regularly check the income and expenditure. Thus, he can make required corrections and control expenditure.

- Record Keeping

"He should check the income and expenditure with reference to the period, place, time, head of income/expenditure, source, bringing forward, quantity, the payer/ paid, the person causing payments to be made, the recorder and the receiver." (2.7.31-32)

Kautilya has recommended maintaining the records of financial transactions in minute detail. He has suggested limiting withdrawals from the treasury. In short, the state should regulate its finance in such a way that it can easily manage through calamitous times.

As an economist, Kautilya balanced his budgets well and always preferred surplus budgets to deficit budgets.

- Taxation

However, while filling up the treasury he was conscious of the economic structure of the people. Several sections of society such as old people, crippled persons, and widows were exempted from taxation.

Kautilya took several steps to ensure that a king got taxes from people like a person picked up ripe fruits from a tree. The king should not anger the people by over-burdening them with taxes, just as one should not pluck unripe fruits as it affects the growth of the tree.

25

Internal Accounting Systems

THE TREASURY IS THE HEART of an organisation. It is always based on the financial performance of the company that is evaluated by its investors, shareholders, and promoters.

Both the CEO (Chief Executive Officer) and the CFO (Chief Financial Officer) ensure that the organisation is in good financial condition. It is important for them to not only build a good internal accounting system, but to also ensure that there are no unwanted expenses. Thus, they ensure that the employees are not corrupt.

In order to achieve this, Kautilya says that a good financial reporting system has to be developed in an organisation. He offers some advice regarding a good accounting system within an organisation:

"In addition to reporting in detail as well as in aggregate, there is also an individual accountability for the revenues and the expenditures." (2.7.24)

Revenues and expenditures are part of the continuous cycle in any economy. A regular record of both has to be maintained. A detailed account of each of the heads of revenues and expenses is to be recorded by the accounts department. The *Arthashastra* deals with this topic, covering this subject from various angles.

Mostly, revenue is received via a single department, but expenditures are made by different departments. Therefore, a detailed as well as collective report of the revenue and expenditures has to be maintained. Expenses have to be recorded not only as heads, but also note the individuals who are responsible for it. In this manner, it is easy to track the outgoing in an organisation, and who is causing it.

"He (leader) should check the accounts for each day, group of five days, fortnight, month, four months (quarterly) and a year." (2.7.30)

Not only do proper records have to be maintained, it is important for the leader to check these on a regular basis. Kautilya lists the periods when these accounts should be checked. He says that the check should be carried out daily, weekly, every 15 days, monthly, quarterly, and yearly.

This system started by Kautilya 2400 years ago has already been widely practised by organisations across the globe. Not only has this principle been applied in the accounting systems, it can be applied in various departments to ensure productivity.

For example, if a sales target, or the deadline for completing a project is set, the leader has to keep checking the progress on a daily, weekly, monthly, quarterly, and yearly basis. This will keep the employees on their toes and the leader alert and active.

Jack Welch, the former head of GE, once said, "Regular reporting and inspections are required in order to get focused and refocused on our goals."

26

Paying Taxes on Time

MARCH SIGNALS THE END of the financial year when people start paying their taxes. Nearly every one is busy filing their returns and/or making investments that offer tax benefits. But should we manipulate our accounts so much that we do not pay taxes at all?

Kautilya says it is the duty of the citizen to pay taxes and that of the leaders to use the taxes for nation building:

"Those who do not pay fines and taxes take on themselves the sins of those (kings) and the kings who do not bring about well-being and security (take on themselves the sins) of the subjects." (1.13.8)

The concept of direct and indirect taxes and also fines was formally introduced and made systematic by Kautilya 2400 years ago! The income of the whole government machinery depends on taxes and fines. The money thus collected is used for national security, maintenance, and development.

Therefore, according to Kautilya, not paying taxes brings on our heads the sins of their leaders and the nation. On the other hand, the kings (politicians and government officials) who misuse the money collected will have to suffer for the sins of the people.

While filing your returns remember these tips:

- Do Not Wait for March

A recent survey showed that over 70 percent employees pay their entire salary for March as taxes. This is only because they postponed the essential. Plan your investments and tax payments in advance. A tax planner once said, "I invest a lakh in the beginning of the financial year, i.e. in April."

- Have a Tax Consultant

Lots of changes related to taxes, constantly take place in the corporate world. Even two years after implementing the Value Added Tax (VAT) and Fringe Benefit Tax (FBT), most company owners do not understand what it entails. Engage an expert tax consultant who can help you understand these concepts.

- Do Not be Afraid

Do not be afraid of inspections by the government. If you have paid your taxes and discharged your duty towards the nation, why should you be afraid of inspections, or routine checks? Fear of government servants leads to corruption.

Let us take an oath to fight corruption. Fighting corruption will not be necessary if one only follows the rules laid down by the Anti-Corruption Bureau. Corrupt people will be caught and punished only when each citizen awakens to the commitment of nation-building. Being fearless is the only way to proceed.

27

Profit Margin

IT IS TAKEN FOR GRANTED that a good business venture, or a well-to-do person, has to have a good financial plan. Even Chanakya, centuries ago, believed that a good 'treasury' is one of the strong pillars that supports successful businesses.

He had suggested,

"He should secure an undertaking requiring little expenditure and yielding large profit and get a special advantage." (7.12.31)

In other words — control the expenses and keep an eye on the net profit or savings.

But how can one become financially successful? Well, these tips will certainly help you:

- Spend Time Budgeting

It is worth spending time on calculations. A businessman would need to calculate the time required for a project and the number of people required. A salaried person would be concerned with his goals and the money to fund it. But, both need to keep an eye on possible miscellaneous expenses. Finally, don't forget to keep some extra money aside as buffer. If you are new to such an exercise then take the help of your seniors, or people who have such experience.

- Keep a Daily Check on Accounts

The discipline of maintaining daily accounts has to be introduced, especially in the face of deadlines and routine activities. It may seem difficult at the start. But, a daily check ensures that one is in control of one's finances. Successful companies and people know exactly how much income has been received daily, how much expense has been made, as well as the balance in the 'treasury'.

- Special Advantage

Earn from your experience. If you are a 'niche' player or a

talented professional, make it a point to take advantage of this and charge extra. Experts have the advantage of being rare in the market and receive a lot of offers. This advantage has to be used! With less time in hand and more to deliver, it is better to charge 'extra' and mark up the profits. We see celebrities doing that. So can you.

- Cash Flow

This is the bottom line — the most important factor. In any business or house, a regular cash flow is required. But the pipeline alone is not important, the conversion is. We have salaries/bills to pay, suppliers to be taken care of, and regular maintenance to be carried out. So be sure of your plan/path and build a model where the cash flow is regular and sustainable.

When financial stability is thus secured, you can take bigger risks, invest in new ventures and gamble a little in unknown areas. For Chanakya this was how a country became prosperous.

28

Proper Accounts

CHANAKYA'S *ARTHASHASTRA* IS AN ancient book that explains financial procedures and systems in detail. Some of the accounting models used by Chanakya are still a wonder to modern finance wizards.

Chanakya emphasised the importance of maintaining regular and daily accounts. For those who mismanage the treasury, the punishments were outlined:

"If the (officer) does not deliver the income that has accrued (or) does not pay the expenses put down in writing (or) denies the balance received, that is misappropriation." (2.8.18)

But how do we maintain regular accounts in our day-to-day life? Well, here are some tips:

- Learn to Write it Down

Money management is about discipline. And only a disciplined man can keep control over his accounts. People withdraw money from ATMs and spend it without having any clue about where it went. If you also do this, you'd better make it a habit to write down your accounts — daily! This should include how much money you had at the start of the day, where you spent it, how much balance was left at the end of the day. Start this exercise — now!

- Analyse It

Just writing down your expenses is not enough. From time to time, look back and take stock. A man who had no clue about where all his money was disappearing did the above exercise. At the end of one month he realised that he was spending nearly 60 percent of his salary on restaurant bills. He understood where his expenses could be cut. He was more aware about each rupee he spent.

- Differentiate between Need and Greed

This is the biggest challenge! While buying things, ask yourself, "Is it my need or greed?" If you want to buy a good pair of shoes — buy it. But if you are buying three pairs because of a discount, that is greed. These days, every consumer faces this challenge frequently. In Gandhiji's beautiful words, "There is enough for everyone's need, but not for one man's greed."

- Be Careful with the Credit Card

A leading financial expert said, "The credit card is the most dangerous invention of mankind!" Truly, the 'Buy now, spend later' philosophy it encourages can be dangerous, unless you pay your bills in time. Else, God save you! Warren Buffet, one of the richest men in the world, has never taken a credit card.

29

Advance Money

EVERY ORGANISATION INCURS fixed expenses to fund day-to-day operations. Their budgets factor in costs incurred on travelling, stationery, office maintenance, power consumption, salaries, etc.

In addition to this, certain people have to be assigned advance money to handle these transactions and make payments. If this is not done, even the most well-established business could trip over minor issues.

At the end of every month, the firm produces an expense statement to show how much of the advance money — known as 'imprest' money in the modern accounting world — has been spent. It's definitely a good idea to pay attention to the smallest detail as it better equips a businessman to analyse costs (for his firm) and even the end price (for customers). This is not a new concept. Even Chanakya referred to it in the ancient accounting system in *Arthashastra* nearly 2400 years ago.

He said,

"The horse attendant shall receive from the treasury and the magazine a month's allowance (for the horse) and carefully look after it." (2.30.3)

The above sutra gives us an insight into how, even two millennia ago, a horse attendant was given enough food and advance money so that the horse under his supervision enjoyed good health and the person in-charge did not suffer.

But how do we adopt this system today? Here are a few tips:

- Factor in Everything

If you set up a new firm using this exercise, you would actually be creating a new system too. So, you need to plan in detail, factoring in all possible expenses including those that are likely to happen in the future. Also, take into account inflation and other price hikes.

- Ask an Expert

Never hesitate to take advice from an expert, like a chartered accountant who has the requisite skills and knowledge. Accept the fact that you may know many things about your business, but the expert knows many businesses like yours. He can suggest more additions.

His insight will help you not repeat mistakes made by others.

- Audit Regularly

Making a system is not enough — using the system is! Therefore, after creating a system, train your employees to use it regularly. Audit it from time to time to ensure that things are in place. This also helps you monitor and direct work in a better manner. You can engage internal auditors and external auditors.

Do remember that any system you employ has to be useful, user-friendly, and able to generate the report you want at the click of a button.

30

Paying Your Taxes

COME FEBRUARY IN INDIA and the entire business community waits for the presentation of the Union Budget. Everyone looks forward to news about any new tax rules or, better still, reforms.

Taxes are an extremely important tool for nation building. It's one of the major revenue streams for any government. The money collected is used for infrastructure, education, health, defence, and other similarly vital sectors.

But, while it's imperative that the government sets tax slabs judiciously, it's also important that all citizens pay their due taxes honestly and punctually.

Even Chanakya had said:

"All experts shall fix revocation in such a way that neither the donor nor the receiver is harmed." (3.16.5)

In the above verse, we find one of the most beautiful words of advice given by Chanakya — the best way of collecting revenue. He stressed that this part of governance should not adversely affect the giver, or the receiver. The giver should be happy to give and the receiver should be able to meet his target.

But why should the giver happily pay his taxes?

- The Nation Needs You

There are people who are better placed financially than others — individuals and companies whose basic requirements are fulfilled. They need to step up and contribute to nation building, making the maximum contribution.

Chanakya has not forgotten the payers' needs too. He had said, "Taxes should be collected the way a honeybee collects honey from the flower." The flower is willing to give up its sweetness, but the bee also takes care that only a little is taken without hurting the flower.

- Why Some Are Not Taxed...

I am sure that, at some point or the other, you may have felt you are being taxed far more than others. But understand that these 'others' are those who have been left behind by society.

These are the financially insecure people who are still struggling to buy such basic needs as food, clothing, shelter, and need a semblance of financial security. Naturally, not only will they require tax exemptions, but also other privileges.

You have to understand that these people, with your tax support, will eventually come up to the first level of paying taxes themselves.

- For Total Development

This is the government's responsibility. While funds need to be allocated taking the human happiness index into account, it should be distributed in such a manner that it helps the total development of the society.

Even arts, sports, literature, and research needs to be supported financially. And if you pay your taxes, you would, basically, be financing them too. It's like the Lebanese-American author Khalil Gibran wrote in *The Prophet*, " ...and if there come the singers and the dancers and the flute players, buy of their gifts also."

Thus, one can support the artists directly, and also indirectly, by paying taxes.

31

Making Timely Payments

BUSINESS IS NOT ABOUT creating only goodwill. Rather, it's about creating real brand value in the hearts of customers, suppliers, and even the employees. One way of doing this is by making timely payments to all vendors and employees.

Chanakya also emphasised the importance of paying wages on time. He even suggested penalising those who didn't:

"In the case of non-payment of the wage, the fine is one-tenth or six panas. In case of denial, the fine is twelve panas or one-fifth." (3.13.33)

This verse highlights the sanctity of an agreement.

Even in today's world, if a person rescinds on making a promised payment after the required work is done, he can be punished under the law of the land.

But, in addition to adhering to the law, a leader has to also understand the benefits one gets by giving people their dues on time:

- A Promise is a Promise

When a company's chairman, or the head of any department or strategic business unit promises something, he represents his entire team. It becomes his responsibility to fulfill the promise.

While defining leadership qualities in the *Arthashastra*, Chanakya had said that one should never 'over-promise' something and then 'under-deliver'. Instead, he said, it's better to 'under-promise' and 'over-deliver'! Of course, the best thing would be to never promise anything, if you are not sure about its execution.

- Be Clear in Financial Dealings

The first rule of business is to look at all financial matters before committing to anything. In fact, you should also apply this rule in your personal life — it will prove to be very beneficial.

If you need a new television, you should first determine what your budget is. For example, if you have only Rs 10,000, then buy a TV that costs that much. It's no use wasting time in showrooms looking at an LCD for Rs 50,000, or breaking your head over consumer loans and EMI schemes. In other words, always work out your financials first, and then accept the deal.

- Have a Clear Conscience

A man of wisdom once said, "The softest pillow is a clear conscience." If you keep your word even in the smallest of deals, you will be able to sleep well.

Of course, there's always a chance of some mis-communication, or minor irritation. However, it's important to discuss and solve these issues in order to restore a good working relationship.

Remember, the real goodwill is the brand you create, and nothing should be allowed to tarnish it.

32

Dirty Money

NARENDRA MODI, CHIEF MINISTER of Gujarat State, was addressing a gathering of businessmen in Mumbai. While he was encouraging investments in Gujarat, Modi said that 'dirty money' was a big danger to the entire economic recession.

Now, dirty money is not the same as 'black money'. The word 'dirty' is used to describe money that is used by such extreme anti-social elements as terrorists and even the Mafia. If we allow its use in the mainstream economy, there will be very bad consequences. Therefore, one of the prime objectives in today's world is to make sure this kind of suspect finance, and the people behind it, are not supported.

Chanakya had said:

"For one calling another, who is not a thief, the punishment shall be that for a thief, also for one hiding a thief." (4.8.6)

Now this verse highlights something important — never ever support wrong-doers. If that happens ("one calling another..."), the situation will become uncontrollable.

Hence, the punishment for such people will be the same as that given to the wrong-doers themselves.

There are some simple things that you can do to avoid such a scenario:

- Deal with the Right People

Regarding business and the work place, it's important to choose the right organisation. Half the battle is won when we work in a good environment and with good people. If you work with suppliers, choose those who display good ethics and right practices. If you are a housewife and are trying to choose a product from two different companies — choose that company which is trustworthy.

- Think Long-Term

This is the biggest solution to most problems. Working with the right people may not give us immediate benefits. But, in the long-term, the returns will be very high.

I know of many people who started working in the right companies and received small roles and salaries. Today, they are well-respected directors. So, choose wisely the company you want to keep and the career you want to build. Do it while keeping the long-term benefits in mind.

- Oppose What is Wrong

If you find out about some wrong practices, stop it. Chanakya made it clear that keeping quiet is a big crime. I know someone who used to file a complaint for every wrong practice he noticed — whether it was a corrupt traffic policeman, or an autorickshaw driver with an extra-fast meter. Today, he is feared by politicians and is an inspiration to the younger generation that is passionate about fighting corruption.

33

Money for Wealth Creation

CHANAKYA HAS TWO FAMOUS works to his credit, the elaborate *Kautilya's Arthashastra* with nearly 6000 verses and *Chankaya Niti*, a key to *Arthashastra* with just 330 one-line verses. Various verses in both the books deal with the principles of creation and the management of wealth.

Kautilya says that money is not wealth. It is just a tool. Wealth is ever present in the universe. Like energy, wealth is constant; it only changes its names and forms. The secret of wealth creation is to understand the movement of wealth from one person to another, from one nation to another, from one generation to another.

Wealth is not only what is 'with' you but also what is 'in' you.

Arthashastra says that the qualities of a person, character, and knowledge are prime requirements for wealth-creation.

It is largely misunderstood that wealth is what is around you. Your car, your house, and other possessions do not constitute real wealth. In fact, they are byproducts of your inner wealth.

The inner wealth of knowledge, experience, and wisdom are your true wealth. Without them, you cannot create external wealth. Only continuous empowerment with knowledge helps wealth flow to you. "A knowledgeable man can create wealth anywhere anytime."

"Be ever active in the management of the economy because the root of wealth is economic activity; inactivity brings material distress. Without an active policy, both current prosperity and future gains are destroyed." (1.19.35-36)

Chanakya says that activity is the root of wealth. An organisation without active strategies, constant information flows, and regular reports cannot sustain itself. A lazy organisation will plunge into distress. Wealth creation is impossible without an active policy. Without an active economic and financial policy, the present hard-earned wealth will be destroyed and there will be no hope for future profits.

Targets, deadlines, and a focused approach are just pointers to keep employees on their toes. A good profitable organisation requires continuous activity, without which wealth will never be attracted towards it. Also, individuals who are lazy will not be able to create wealth.

34

Money for More Money

"THE OBJECTIVE OF ANY KING (LEADER) or state (organisation) is to create, expand, protect and enjoy wealth." (Book 1, Chapter 1)

The role of a CEO is very clearly defined by Kautilya at the very start of the *Arthashastra*. It is to create wealth for all the stakeholders of the organisation, the employees, and for himself to enjoy.

He should not be satisfied with what he has got. He should constantly think about how to expand his territories and reach new markets.

"Just as elephants are needed to catch elephants, so does one need wealth to capture more wealth." (9.4.27)

This is an old, but very important aspect, of wealth creation — *paisa lagaye bina paisa nahin aata* (there is no business that can create wealth without any investment). The example Kautilya gives here is that of a hunter who catches elephants.

Elephants always move around in groups. To catch an elephant, a hunter needs to use another elephant. Only then will the targeted one be lured away and caught.

Having produced wealth, the king should know how to protect it. If, for instance, we have a vessel with a hole at the bottom, we may keep pouring more and more water into it. However, no water will stay in it unless it is protected from the leak.

How does one do this?

"He (leader) should constantly hold an inspection of their works, men being inconstant in their minds." (2.9.2-3)

The employees are primarily concerned with their salaries. An attitude of complacency can crop up if a regular and vigilant check is not kept on them. The reason is quite obvious. The human mind is very unpredictable. No organisation can reach its goal without a continuous push and pull system.

"All state activities depend first on the Treasury. Therefore, a king (leader) shall devote the best attention to it." (2.8.1-2)

In Book One of the *Arthashastra* titled *The Topic of*

Training, the teacher proposes a daily time table for the king. He says that during the first part of the day, he should check the accounts of income and expenditures of the state. It is only after doing this that he is advised to look into the affairs of the citizens.

Do not get carried away by the regular problems faced by your subordinates once you enter your office. Relax! Just take control of the financial status by monitoring the financial reports first.

35

Road to Wealth

GO RURAL, IS THE THEME of every big corporation today. While FMCG companies eagerly wait for the post-monsoon rural demand to boost their sales, banks, which now sell myriad financial products, are gradually realising the potential of rural areas. Several corporations are re-orienting their growth strategies — ITC's e-choupal and Hindustan Lever's Project Shakti for example — to bring villages into the centre of their plans.

Kautilya was inspired by this principle when managing his treasury.

"Wealth and power comes from the countryside, which is the source of all activities." (7.14.19)

Going rural has two benefits. First, the countryside is the place where raw material is available in plenty. Minerals, food crops, labour all find their sources in the countryside. Second, it is also a ready market for high-volume business.

Even today, India lives in the villages. Be it the soft drinks, the mobile phones, or the insurance industry, all have already tried to penetrate the rural sector.

In the Book 2 of the *Arthashastra*, Chapter 8, Verse 3, Kautilya points out various elements which contribute to the increase in the treasury:

- Increase in Commerce and Trade

Commercial activities recycle the wealth of a nation. It helps the wealth flow from one sector to the other, from one geographical area to another. Trading helps in wealth being circulated from one nation to another. Exports and imports are the lifeline of any economically developing nation.

- Arresting Perpetrators of Crime

Monitoring and controlling theft is essential. A system of checks and counter checks are necessary to protect the treasury. Theft can be an inside job, or can be influenced by external elements.

- Reduction in Establishment

Expenses can be controlled by reducing the size of the organisation. This is done by keeping the minimum required employees, as well as reducing the number of liabilities. Outsourcing is one of the best ways of controlling the overheads of a company.

- Plenty of Crops

Even today, India is an agriculture-based economy. A lot depends on the monsoons. Investment in R&D in this sector to increase crop yields, better warehousing of agricultural produce, and food processing, could add significantly to the growth of the economy.

- Plenty of Marketable Goods

Sales and marketing should be supplied with enough products. Availability of stocks at the right time, sales order processing, logistics and distribution have to be in place to ensure the achievement of any sales target.

- Freedom from Calamities

A lot of unseen and unknown factors affect the economy of a nation, organisation, and also individuals. The board of directors should consider all these aspects, under the 'Risk Management Plan' of an organisation. Insurance, savings, and good investment plans are the steps taken to ensure freedom from calamities.

Teamwork

36

Security and Monitoring Systems

EVERYONE KNOWS HOW IMPORTANT security is. Still, most people do not maintain a proper monitoring and vigilance system, although it can avoid, or at least immensely contain and confine, leaks. Without a proper security system, processes will get out of control one day and this could be fatal for the organisation.

Chanakya has devised systems for the security and protection of goods in an organisation. He says,

"Every object should go out of, or come into (the palace), after it is examined and its arrival or departure is recorded." (1.20.23)

In an office there are many transactions taking place daily. People come in and go out, goods are delivered, some are sent out. Such exchanges are more common in manufacturing sectors, like factories, and other production units.

Chanakya has clearly noted the importance of good strict security procedures systems and documentation of all goods-related transactions in the organisation. He also suggests that, before they are recorded, the information should be examined to ensure that what is recorded is correct and genuine.

How do we follow this advice in today's corporate scenario? Here are some suggestions:

- Use Technology

We now have various gadgets and equipments that easily record and document all transactions. Cameras perched on top of gates for surveillance, bar-coding for tracking goods and other such systems/processes can make things easy and save a lot of time. Technology also has the added advantage of reducing human errors.

- Make Your System Unique

Even though there are various readymade software packages available in the market for security purposes, make sure that you pick the one that records all the things that are important and useful to *you*. If need be, get a tailor-made system in order to get the required reports as quick as possible.

- Monitor the System

Just setting up a working system will not ensure its smooth functioning. Make sure that you, as a manager, keep checking the system at regular intervals. In this way, the security personnel — and even the general staff will always be on their toes.

- Conduct Surprise Inspections

This is the most effective way to keep security under your control. Keep a close (and unannounced) watch on the people who handle your security systems. Subject them to surprise checks. At times, it is also important to transfer security personnel without giving them any notice.

Finally, do remember that security is not just about having technology in place. Rather, security is about you being alert and vigilant all the time, for all the required processes. After all, like a leading consultancy once noted to its dismay, "It just doesn't work if you check all the visitors and their bags on the way in, but hardly ever when they are going out!"

37

Right Business Partner

IN TODAY'S CORPORATE WORLD, getting funds is not really a problem. The Indian market is flooded with money for anyone who comes up with good ideas.

Of course, in the initial stages while struggling, a new businessman may think his idea is not good. However, if he strongly believes in his own idea and continues to put in efforts, the situation will change eventually. He will even find many people who are ready to finance his company. This is when he gets opportunities for finding a new and financially stronger partner. However, when such offers come flooding in, the challenge is to choose the right partner.

Chanakya advises,

"If situated between two stronger kings, he should seek shelter with one capable of protecting him." (7.2.13)

So, when multiple potential partners arrive with a lot of money and experience, you should be very alert and cool-headed. After all, a wrong choice can ruin the business that you have created from scratch.

To make the correct choice, one should be able to evaluate each potential partner's strengths and only then tie up with the one who is strongest. Here are a few tips to determine who will be the right partner.

- Consider Your Values

Business is about the values you follow. Each person invests his feelings, hopes, and emotions into the organisation. When a new partner enters the picture, it is important to consider if your values and his values match. Both parties should have the same wavelength.

- The Long-Term Approach

At times, one may impulsively accept funds when it's readily available. But consider all possibilities, and devise a long-term strategy before you tie up with anyone. Else, the situation will resemble that of a person who has been looking for a spouse for a long time, and as soon as anyone says 'yes', the person will get married, only to realise later that this was the greatest blunder in his/her life! So check your partner's credentials with known sources before the partnership becomes legal. It may take some time, but you will be the winner in the long run.

- It's Not Just Money

Partnerships are not just about money. It is not just plain give-and-take. In fact, it is about a life-long relationship that needs to be worked upon. As Stephen Covey says in his book, *Seven Habits of Highly Effective People*, "....you need to develop an emotional bank account." You will have to spend time with your partners regularly. It is necessary to communicate with them so that the relationship strengthens beyond just business transactions.

Remember, every business story is the story of building the right team to work with and being able to work together. No wonder then that choosing the right team members is highly important to win the game.

38

Effective Meetings

MEETINGS, MEETINGS, AND MORE meetings! As you climb higher up the corporate ladder, and your business grows, meetings will become an inevitable part of your life.

Meetings are like a double-edged sword — they are either a waste of your time, or you can scale up your business. It all depends on how effective you are in conducting meetings.

Chanakya gives us some tips on this issue:

"He should declare without loss of time what is in the king's interest." (5.4.11)

The following are also some tips that can help you in meetings:

- Have an Agenda

Most meetings are a big drain on one's time, because there is no clear agenda. The purpose of the meeting has to be clear. The best meetings are those that take into consideration the vision of the company, or what is of interest to the seniors.

Preparing an agenda gives a sense of direction to the meeting. If you have called for the meeting, then ensure that the agenda is clearly communicated to others. Also, ensure maximum attendance and least confusion by telling the participants in advance about the day, time, and venue of the meeting.

As Bill Gates wrote it in his book, *Business at the Speed of*

Thought, "Those meetings that are planned well in advance are the most effective ones."

- Give Direction

You can be open for a brainstorming session, or a discussion. But that should not allow the meeting to go astray. As a chairperson, you need to give the meeting a sense of direction.

You have to be like a good televison talk-show anchor — when the answers to any question are going off-track, or if the person being questioned is talking too much, you cut him off diplomatically, and move to the next question.

- Come to the Point, ASAP!

This is very critical. Meetings need to be started off like any other session. Be casual — ask the team about the status of the project, find out if there are any issues, offer tea, start the discussion, etc.

However, as the meeting proceeds, it is very necessary to come to the point as soon as possible, ASAP! We have to monitor our time.

Therefore, the success of any meeting lies in having only a few and important points in the agenda. Most importantly, as the meetings come to the end, make an action plan. Take decisions and execute them. Otherwise it will be like the old office joke, "When our boss has nothing to do, he calls for a meeting!"

39

Planning a Business Trip

TRAVELLING IS A VERY IMPORTANT part of business development. It helps you approach new clients, try new markets, and get feedback on new products and services that your firm may be experimenting with.

In today's globalised corporate world, travelling across the country, or even across continents, is an essential part of any business. Exploring new business development opportunities, reaching new investors or seeking Joint Ventures (JV) are common and important tasks even in small-sized companies.

But planning for your business travel is an equally important task. Chanakya gives us a hint:

"He should start after making proper arrangements for vehicles, draught-animals and retinue of servants." (1.16.5)

Here are some additional tips to be kept in mind while planning for your business trip:

- Have a Clear Travel Plan

It is important to make a clear travel plan — complete with an itinerary for the number of days you will be in the new region. Take into consideration the requirement of time, money, and various other factors. Use local contacts to make your plan clear and precise. Leave some extra time to explore any unexpected opportunities.

- Your Travelling Team

Who are the people travelling with you? How many? What are their roles? These are some important questions that need to be answered. A team also adds strength to your mission. That is why government officials always travel with a delegation.

- Study Potential Prospective Targets Well

Even before you leave, study the prospective target. Most of the basic information will be available on the internet. Verify the information through trusted sources. When face-to-face with them, ask them specific questions to make sure all the information is correct. After all, if you are looking at a long-term association you need to make sure you are signing a deal with the right partner.

- Do Not Close Deals Immediately

At times, it is very exciting to close deals in the very first meeting. Resist this temptation. All that glitters is not gold. The first impression need not necessarily be the lasting impression. Come back home. Then, with a cool mind, restudy all the important areas and, with the help of experts, take the next step.

Remember, while every new opportunity is a possibility, it is important to do a little bit of thinking so that you can handle future events better. You should aim to be like the successful businessman who was once offered a billion dollars as investment in his company. Quick came his reply, "Thanks for the offer, will get back to you soon!"

40

Public Relations

PETER DRUCKER, THE well-known management guru, had once remarked that one of the top priorities of a business leader is to network, socialise, and maintain great PR (Public Relations). "It's all about great relationships that you maintain with your clients, suppliers, shareholders, employees, and every other person you come in contact with!"

Even our own ancient guru and probably the first management thinker, Chanakya, brought out the same idea in his book of advice for kings and other leaders,

"He should establish contacts with forest chieftains, frontier-chiefs, and chief officials in the cities and the countryside." (1.16.7)

But, how to build a network and maintain contacts is an art every leader has to develop. Here are some tips:

- Attend Meetings

For a CEO, not a single day should go by without meeting at least one new person. He must attend business conferences, training programmes or even one-to-one meetings with important people. In addition to making contacts, he should even start learning from the experiences of others.

- Keep in Touch

Collecting contact details may not be enough. Most of us return from various conferences with a pile of visiting cards and do nothing about it. Hence, a follow-up with each important person is a must. Think of the business possibilities with each person you met and work out a proposal.

- Two-Way Approach

Most businessmen go wrong by thinking only of the benefits that he will get from the new contact! Rather, think about how you will be able to help them. At times, you can offer a tip or suggestion that will scale up their business. Help them, and probably, they will help you when you need them.

- Long-Term Approach

In human relationships, time is important and in business 'timing' is important. But to know the right timing, you have to spend enough time. Never spoil any potential business relationship just because it may not appear to be immediately beneficial. One has to always think about the long-term. Take it slow, but sure. You never know. A person who seems small today may become a giant tomorrow, while a giant today may be out on the streets later.

Always remember that while leadership is an art, business is a far more superior art. It requires the understanding of people, understanding their minds, and also understanding the various factors that fulfill each person. Thus, in business, PR cannot be done by just outsourcing it to an agency. You may have a PR agency if required, and your personal involvement, your time, and effort must be invested wisely.

41

Honour Men with Qualities

A SHARP PERSON KNOWS HOW to differentiate between ordinary men and great men. And if a leader can successfully inculcate this quality, he can easily become victorious in all walks of life. Just like a jeweler does, one should have the knack of differentiating between rare gems and ordinary stones.

According to Chanakya, the greatest resource a business has, is the workforce. In fact, people are the source of all great achievements, all of which are performed by men who have great qualities.

And it's these qualities that have to be recognised and honoured. Chanakya, while defining these qualities, had said,

"Men are to be honoured on account of excellence in learning, intellect, valour, noble birth, and deeds." (3.20.23)

In other words, men of each type have to be honoured in any organisation. Let us look at each type separately:

- Men of Learning

Men of learning are the most respected people in every society. Other than academic and scholarly learning, this description also relates to men having the wisdom of experience.

In India, especially, we have always held men of learning in very high esteem. A sociologist had once said, "A society that does not respect men of learning is bound to collapse."

- Valour

The brave. The fighters. They have that extra quality in them to 'go on', in spite of problems. They are even ready to face death, if required. Such people are called Kshatriyas. They are the soldiers and guards who protect us. As the armies say, "We keep awake in the nights so that all of you can sleep peacefully."

- Noble Birth

Persons born in noble families are automatically respected. Now this is not being caste-biased or racist. However, we find that certain qualities are genetic. The family background also influences the personality of a person.

- Deeds

Finally, your actions speak louder than your words. What you achieve will automatically command respect. Therefore, men who have done great and noble deeds need to be respected too.

When you identify such persons, you can associate with them and learn from them. You will then find that the benefits you get can be plotted on an upward sloping curve.

This is especially true in the world of business. It is said that J.R.D. Tata was able to identify 'quality men'. He made them part of his team, and the Tatas have been succeeding for generations.

42

A Good Meeting

BILL GATES HAD SAID IN HIS BOOK, *Business At The Speed Of Thought*, "The most effective meetings are the ones in which the participants come well-prepared."

This is true, and Chanakya had made this a rule a long time ago in our country. He wanted people to not only be punctual for meetings, but also be well-prepared with reports.

If they turned up without reports, they were actually fined, or even punished.

He said,

"For (managers) not coming at the proper time, or coming without the account books and balances, the fine shall be one-tenth of the amount due." (2.7.21)

Disciplined behaviour during meetings is very important. Chanakya also listed other important aspects of a well-prepared meeting.

• Why Have a Meeting?

A meeting is an event where two or more people meet to discuss certain ideas. In a company, most meetings have an agenda. For example, a sales review meeting. This will require the sales team to get together and discuss the targets achieved, upcoming strategies to meet the next targets and also the plans for moving ahead.

A meeting is also held to exchange ideas, it is an opportunity to network, understand the working styles of others as well as to share, or seek, information.

- The Benefits of a Good Meeting

A good meeting is one that has a clear agenda. The timing for such meetings is worked out well in advance and communicated to all. It starts on time and also ends on time. People feel good after such a productive meeting, rather than feel frustrated at having to sit through one meeting flowing into another without any progress being made.

In today's scenario especially, when time is a precious commodity, one should not call for a meeting without a clear agenda. Every second has to be productive.

- Preparing for a Good Meeting

The first thing one must prepare is what needs to be communicated. This is the role of the organiser. Remember, you have to communicate four things to the relevant participants way before they even get together — where, when, who, and what.

Where is the meeting going to be held (venue). When (the time, both start and end times), who (the chairperson, or speaker, for the session), and what (the agenda and the topic for the meeting).

In any event, if you are a participant in the meeting, you must always come prepared with relevant reports and required papers.

When asked for any particular information, no time should be wasted. A quick and prompt response will help the decision-making process.

Additionally, try to understand the importance of a meeting. Be a good organiser, conductor, and participant. Also, never hesitate to teach others the importance of effective meetings.

43

Finish What You Have Started

I HAVE A FRIEND WHO SEEMS destined to end each and every project he takes up with nothing but success. I once asked him to share his secret with me.

He said, "Before taking on any new project, I always complete the previous work I have undertaken. That ensures that I single-mindedly, and successfully, finish every project I take up!"

These words immediately reminded me of a verse by Chanakya:

"Activity is that which brings about the accomplishment of works undertaken." (6.2.2)

Very few people are good at completing the work they have already started. Indeed, almost all of us keep on taking new projects, accept new orders and even pick up new books to read without asking ourselves, "Shouldn't I first complete the existing one?"

No wonder we land up with various problems like stress, atrocious time-management, and a pathetic work-life balance. Why don't we first complete the work we already have at hand?

Chanakya says that this happens because we are not 'active'. We have to 'act' to complete all existing work. There's simply no alternative to this.

And you only need to remember a few steps:

- List All Pending Work

If you want to see why your life is in a mess, try this

simple exercise — list the number of activities that you have started, but not completed, or finished, till date.

It could be finishing a report, calling up and thanking the organisers of an event, or simply completing that book you picked up. If you're honest, you will be shocked at the size of your list!

- Plan it, and Do It

Now, list the time required for completing each unfinished work. For example, it may take half an hour to finish that report. Or about 5-10 minutes to call and thank the organisers of that party. Or the book that you started reading and left mid-way may take about three hours more to finish.

Keep some time aside, say about an hour daily, to complete these unfinished tasks. More importantly, you must actually do it! Don't just think about doing it.

- Make it a Habit

This exercise may look difficult initially. After all, we all do get into the dirty habit of procrastinating. But if we really discipline ourselves by completing all unfinished tasks, our self-confidence will grow and we will even yearn for bigger challenges.

The chairman of a multinational firm once revealed to me that he spends his Saturdays just completing any work that may have been left unfinished. This shows how important it is to be a good 'finisher' rather than just being a good 'starter'.

44

Want to Succeed?

KAUTILYA'S *ARTHASHASTRA* COMPRISES fifteen books. Of these, the sixth book has only two chapters. Yet, it's very important as it explains how a king can run his kingdom successfully. It also lists the three ways to succeed and how we can do it.

Chanakya had said:

"Success is threefold — that attainable by the power of counsel is success by counsel, that attainable by the power of might is success by might, that attainable by the power of energy is success by energy." (6.2.30)

While it takes a lifetime full of valuable experience to understand the meaning of these words, we can at least understand its essence:

- Succeed by Counsel

There are many people who try and keep trying, and still don't succeed. Frustrated, they believe it's not in their destiny to succeed. But they might have just not got the right advice from the right person.

I remember a foreigner who was trying to set up a business here and could not get started for nearly two years. He finally approached a legal advisor who gave him just a few tips, and he was off!

This accurately portrays the first kind of success which, according to Chanakya, is achieved by listening to, and learning from, the right experts.

- Succeed by Might

When we fight our battles alone, the chances of winning are less. "Together we grow," a spiritual master had once rightly said. Therefore, the second method is to succeed by might — i.e., by the power of association.

I have a friend who is into politics. He always rues the fact that he had to spend a lot of time trying to understand just how politics worked.

"I wish I had a Godfather who would guide me," he once confessed. That's as close to the truth as you will get in today's highly competitive world. In life, if we get to associate with a powerful person, success is virtually guaranteed.

- Succeed by Energy

There are quite a few people who, even if they cannot achieve success via the first two methods, still succeed driven purely by their energy and dynamism. Their enthusiasm is very contagious too. They have a 'never give up' spirit. For them, life is not about how many times one fails. Rather, it's about the feeling — "Success is just a step away!"

They learn from their mistakes, from books, from every person they meet and from every event in their life. Life is a journey for them, and never a destination.

Remember, success is an attitude a person develops. So never give up till you achieve your goal. Chanakya had said, "Even after a hundred trials, an enthusiastic man will surely succeed."

45

Working Together

IN THE 1970s AND 80s, many Indian companies were gearing up to landmark events. Globalisation had not yet begun. Computers were just being introduced, and mobile phones and the Internet were still ideas. Those were the days when the biggest challenge Indian industries faced were labour problems. Misunderstandings between the various labour unions and the company management occurred all the time.

Obviously, not all negotiations produced positive results. Many companies succumbed to those tense situations, eventually shutting down, with entire industries suffering. Only a few organisations emerged as winners.

A key question often asked then was — is it possible to have complete co-operation between unions and managements?

Well, even the experts weren't sure of an answer. However, Chanakya had a solution.

He had said:

"And without informing the employer, the union shall not remove anyone or bring in anyone." (3.14.15)

So, in Chanakya's time, while a union had to be completely in line with the wishes of the management, they also consulted each other before taking decisions.

So what are the lessons our generation can learn from this?

- Unions Will Exist

Today, many management thinkers feel that the 'days of the union' are over. This is not true. Only the name and form changes. What is a union? It's a group of people coming together on a common platform. They discuss their issues together and put forward their proposals to their seniors.

This exists even today. Look at the various committees and groups in any company. As any seasoned corporate official will admit, things flow smoothly only after such problems and issues are sorted out early.

- Need for a Common Vision

Whichever corporate office or industry we work in, we have to realise that we are not fighting against each other, but against the bigger enemies. Therefore, it's important for the top leaders to communicate, to the whole organisation, the company's objectives and goals. This will help everyone in the company — including not just the seniors but also the juniors — share a common vision.

- Regular Communication

One's responsibility doesn't end with just informing the workforce about policies and developments once in a blue moon. As with any relationship, the strength lies in regular and effective communication.

Even though there could be hierarchies and different levels in an organisation, it's important to meet everyone from time to time and discuss issues and problems.

This becomes the firm's strength. No outsider is required to solve a problem if people inside the house are completely in tune with each other.

In the end, remember that it's not 'I' that should win, but that 'we all' should win with the right methods and for the right purpose.

46

Get Everyone Involved

PROBLEMS ARE ALWAYS CROPPING up in any organisation. The moment a problem crops up, all the employees need to think about how it can be solved, rather than just sit and worry about it. They should never expect that the solution will always come from a particular person, department, or group of people.

Chanakya had a suggestion for this:

"He should fight with the mobilisation of all troops." (12.1.3)

In other words, the entire office team has to come together when fighting a problem. For example, if your company's sales figures are affected, don't expect only the sales and marketing department to look into the issue. Call key persons from all departments and brainstorm the issue together. You will then see a different, possibly better, approach to the problem.

Here's a step-by-step process for solving problems together:

- Identify the Problem

Before solving a problem, identify, and understand it thoroughly. It's just like a medical diagnosis which is necessary to identify the root cause of an ailment and find the required medicine.

Thus, if challenged with problems as varied as attrition, financial issues, sales targets or any other, first identify where the problem started.

- Think from Different Perspectives

Do not assume that your first diagnosis is correct. Take a second opinion. It would be even better if you called for a meeting of all senior people. For example, if the manufactured goods are not up to the mark, do not just blame the production team. Instead, call all the department heads — like purchase, R&D, and even sales — and ask them for their opinion on how the issue can be solved. This will help you attack the problem from different perspectives.

- Create a Task Force

Now, after analysing the problem, it's important to fight it till it goes away completely. You have to create a team, or a task force for this as a lone person can get demotivated tackling it alone.

Another advantage of a team is that any of its members can take a break, or rest, for some time, while the others continue brainstorming, this will help maintain morale.

Remember, the whole dynamics of a battle changes when the entire army is focused on winning the battle, no matter who is crowned the 'best warrior'. The secret of team work that guarantees success is that each individual has to surrender to the higher goal.

47

Power of Communication

A BUSINESS SCHOOL CONDUCTED a survey of its former students' careers, grading them 20 years after they completed the course. Surprisingly, the successful ones were not the toppers, but those who knew how to work in teams and, more importantly, had good communication skills.

Chanakya knew the power of communicating well. In fact, he highlighted how it's even easy to use words as a weapon, and how to avoid this from happening:

"Defamation, vilification, and threat constitute verbal injury." (3.18.1)

When you get down to it, you realise that every person requires 'appreciation'. If you cannot appreciate others, you certainly cannot indulge in the opposite:

- Defamation

It means to defame or insult a person. This is used often as a tool by people to get public support. Politicians, celebrities and well-known people always use and abuse 'defamation'. Any top-level official in an organisation also becomes a soft target for defamation. Basically, it questions the credibility and goodwill of the person. You should never defame anyone, unless and until you have your facts right.

- Vilification

This means backbiting. But you should remember this rule, "If you want to appreciate someone — do it in front of others; if you want to tell him about his wrongdoings, do it when he is alone."

Backbiting does not solve any problem. In fact, it's a sign of a weak person. If you feel there is something wrong, go and explain this directly to the person concerned and also tell them why you feel the situation needs to be corrected.

You see, backbiting creates a lot of negative energy which is harmful not only to the person targeted, but also to the one who does it, as well as those who listen to it. This has to be avoided.

- 'Threat'

This means warning a person and trying to infuse fear into him. While phrases like, 'Do this, or else...' are commonly used by competing youngsters, in the adult world it is considered a crime to threaten anyone.

Never try to infuse fear into a person. The reason is that not only does this constitute a crime in the eyes of the law, but for you in the long-term you never know when the person will find the strength to hit back.

The best way to communicate is in a soft, yet firm, manner. Chanakya had once said, "When you communicate, it should be *Satyam* and *Priyam*, i.e. being truthful in a nice manner."

Develop these qualities to succeed in life.

48

Stopping Fights

THE HUMAN MIND IS VERY unpredictable. At times, it gets attached to certain ideas and becomes obstinate about it. Then, when someone else comes along with a conflicting idea, it leads to some kind of friction, and may even result in a fight.

Such behaviour can be very destructive if not controlled at the initial stages. Interpersonal rivalries, corporate battles, wars between countries — all rarely leave even the most neutral party untouched.

Hence, fights have to be stopped, especially group conflicts, and this can be done only with the help of group psychology.

Chanakya, a master psychologist, had a solution:

"Strife among subjects can be averted by winning over the leaders among the subjects, or by removal of the cause of strife." (8.4.18)

Let us take this advice step-by-step:

- Identify the Problem

When a fight occurs, it immediately distorts the region's peace and a lot of time and energy is wasted.

As a strategist, it's important to end the fight and move on in life. However, to do this, it's essential to deeply analyse the situation from all angles and find the root cause of the problem. You need to plan a tentative solution, if not a permanent solution, to end the present fight.

- Talk to Group Leaders

Ask any police officer how they try to calm things down during riots and they will tell you that the first step is to get the warring factions talking.

But it may not be easy to tackle a group of hundred people, if all of them are marching towards you on the streets.

The solution is to identify who the group leaders and influencers are. Call them out separately and talk to them. If the leader is convinced, the whole group comes under control.

It's like shutting down a machine in an emergency — instead of switching off hundreds of buttons, it's better to put off the main switch to deactivate the entire set.

- Solve the Problem

Do not spend all your energy on just discussions and debates — peace has to be achieved. So the aim should not be forgotten — solve the main problem and end the fight.

In the *Arthashastra*, Chanakya talks about the theories of *Sama* (discussions), *Dana* (offering of rewards), *Danda* (punishments) and *Bheda* (creating a split). You can use these methods alternatively, as the situation demands it, to achieve your goal.

49

Teamwork

THE MOST SUCCESSFUL companies, organisations and groups have one thing in common — the ability to ignore individual differences and work as a 'team'. Teamwork is the most essential ingredient that helps groups achieve various goals in spite of various ups and downs.

The leader may be talented and capable as an individual, but he cannot achieve his goals without the help of an efficient team. As one goes up the management ladder, the leader realises that, the most important role of the captain is to 'lead' a good team. He needs to delegate and share his responsibilities with other efficient team members. Apart from his own performance, he needs to play the role of a strategist.

Kautilya warns leaders, who think they can manage on their own without the help of others, about their folly:

"Rulership can be successfully carried out (only) with the help of associates. One wheel alone does not turn. Therefore, he should appoint ministers and listen to their opinion." (1.7.9)

Good generals have good lieutenants. Good CEOs have good managers. They complement each other. As the vehicle cannot run on one wheel, similarly a CEO cannot perform without good managers.

There are a lot of hidden benefits of good teamwork:

- No One is Indispensable

Too much dependency on one person is very dangerous.

However, if we have a good team, his absence is made up by another talented or skilled person. It not only eliminates dependency but also keeps everyone on their toes performing well.

- Individual Weaknesses Are Covered Up

Everyone makes mistakes. But these must be seen as lessons. Other team members perform their best to cover up the loss. In the end, the total result matters, not the individual achievements.

- Individual Strengths Become 'Total' Strength

Each person has his own strengths. Now, these individual strengths collectively become more powerful. Remember the concept of synergy? One plus one is greater than two. One always performs better as a team rather than as individuals.

- You Think Along with Others

Each person has a different understanding of the same situation. Take the opinion of the team members with the help of a little brainstorming. Thus, one thinks about a solution with the help of another person's mind.

As Stephen Covey says, "Strength lies in differences, not in similarities."

Thus, one thinks of a solution to a problem with the help of another person's mind. Therefore, it is important for a leader to appoint the right managers, listen to their opinions and proceed with a certain strategic plan.

Theodore Roosevelt, the 26th president of the United States was once asked about teamwork, "The best executive is the one who has sense enough to pick good men to do what he wants done, and self-restraint enough to keep from meddling with them while they do it," he said.

This also takes a lot of pressure off, and unwanted expectations from, the leader.

50

Brainstorming

MANY MANAGEMENT WORDS and jargon currently used in the modern corporate world define actions that were practised in India ages ago. One of them is the concept of 'brainstorming'.

Kautilya in the *Arthashastra* gives us a step-by-step formula on how to conduct a brainstorming session. Brainstorming can be used not only for crisis management, but also for the creation of new ideas and innovative thinking. Kautilya's tips can also be followed by project managers who want to effectively use the skills of their team members.

He says,

"In an urgent matter, he should call together the councillors as well as the council of ministers and ask them what the majority among them declare or what is conducive to the success of the work, that he (leader) should do." (1.15.58-59)

- Call for a Meeting

Whenever there is any important or urgent matter to be resolved, the first step is to call for a meeting of the team members and advisors. One can involve not only the managers, but also the non-managerial staff, as well as external experts in the discussion.

- Ask Them

The leader should be very clear about the 'particular issue' that he is seeking a solution for. If the important issue is not brought into 'focus' properly, it will be like a blind person leading the blind. One finds that without direction it does not matter how many meetings are planned, they will all end up as a waste of time. Therefore 'ask' everyone the right questions.

- Take the Input of the Majority

What the maximum people in the group consider to be the ideal solution should be taken into consideration. The leader should also take note of the smallest suggestion, even if it may not be applicable in the current situation. May be these small suggestions will be useful to solve some other problem.

- Decide if the Majority is Right

Just because the majority has a particular opinion it may not necessarily be right. Therefore, Kautilya says the final decision of what should be the next step, should be decided only by the leader. While creating an action plan, he should consider what is conducive to the success of the work. Finally everything is dependent on the 'results' not just on the generation of ideas.

Akio Morita, the founder of Sony wanted to create the first ever VHS video tape. For months he brainstormed with his team what the 'size' of such a video tape should be. This led to no clear solution.

One day, out of frustration, he threw a book on the center

of the table. "I want the tape to be of this size. I don't care how you do it". In a few months, the first VHS tape was out in the market — the size of that book!

51

Teaming Up to Succeed

WORKING IN A TEAM IS BETTER than working alone — this is the key to success when it comes to working on a project. Chanakya puts the same thought in the following verse,

"Let us two build a fort." (7.12.1)

Man is a social animal and requires the help of others to survive. From a 'competitive mindset' one should move to a 'compatibility mindset'. Leaders should develop the ability to work in teams and also inspire their teams to work together. And this applies to all the facets of life, at the workplace, in a competitive market and even while managing home affairs.

- Discuss the Project before You Start

Better to involve, than just inform. If you are going to take up a new assignment, call your people and tell them about it. "What do you feel? Is there a better way to do it?" The suggestions and opinions will help you look at the project from different angles. Sometimes the best ideas come from the bottom, even a child's simple ideas can be highly beneficial.

- Show the Direction, but Let Them Walk

As a team leader this is your most important role. Tell them where to go and when to reach there. Let them decide which route to take. Give them the freedom to complete the work their way. Most leaders have a major problem in this regard. 'When I did it the last time, I did it this way, and you also should do it this way!' the leaders think. There are better ways of doing things. Try to adapt to change.

- Do Not Lose Focus

Just by giving them the direction and freedom is not enough. As a leader, one should closely watch developments. Be around when the team requires you. Be focused and help them get refocused. A team should take regular stock of the situation and realise whether it is doing the right things, or not. If the leader does not do this, he will regret later because, he might have started to head north and reached the south. Keep looking at your compass.

- Enjoy Together

The journey itself is the destination. Remember, happiness is not in 'then and there' but lies in the 'now and here'. Do not forget to enjoy the journey. Have fun while working together. Share the team's joys and sorrows. Stress is the result of not taking breaks and sharing burdens.

When you succeed — celebrate! In case you lose, get up again, and move ahead. As it goes, "In happiness and sorrow, in illness and health, in good moments and sad — *together* we shall be."

52

Common Purpose

LIFE IS ALL ABOUT PARTNERSHIPS — be it between spouses, friends, or even business associates. Many relationships work, and many don't. So what is it that differentiates a successful partnership from unsuccessful ones?

Chanakya gives a very clear idea about the same. He says it's the 'common purpose':

"Being not restricted as to place and time and because of having a common purpose, allied troops are better than alien troops." (9.2.17)

Look into your own life, and you will find the above verse to be very true. Whenever you get a partnership offer, always think about the possibilities of failure before you strike a deal. Have an open discussion to identify what is possible and what is not possible.

Now, without much experience, how does one decide whether a particular partnership will work well or not? Here are some thoughts you can dwell on before tying the 'knot':

- Define Your Purpose

First things first — what do you want in life? What are your core values, your purpose, your goals and objectives, your vision, your life's mission? All these are very important parameters within which an individual operates. If, as an individual, you are not clear about your purpose, then you are only confusing yourself and you will end up confusing even those you work with. So define these areas well and create a road-map to achieve the targets. If you have never done this exercise, take a pen and write down your purpose in life now. It will give you a tremendous focus.

- Have an Open Discussion

Once you are clear about what you want, it becomes easy to discuss your goals and objectives with another person. Have a very open discussion. As you are selling your ideas, also listen to the ideas of the person you are discussing with. Keep looking at the common objectives at a strategic level. If you find that there are areas that are common between the two of you, then there's scope for further discussion.

- Give Time to Each Other

Before you sign the MoU (Memorandum of Understanding), give yourself some time. Think things through. Look at all the things that can possibly go wrong, as well as all those things that can go right. Be realistic. Have a long-term view.

Now, before you finally take things forward, comes the most important part. If at the end of all this you still feel that the deal is not workable, be unemotional, and be ready to walk out. An initial uncomfortable feeling is better than suffering all life long.

In leadership and management, the most important thing is what you do *not* do, rather than what you do. So strike the right chord and have a wonderful partnership.

Strategy

53

Requirement of Information

DUE TO THE RAPID GROWTH in the Information Technology (IT) industry, any information is now available in a split second. Online search engines, mobile phones, radio, television, and newspapers also add to the ready availability of information at the speed of thought.

However, one wonders if all kinds of information are really useful, or is it just junk that is being dumped on us. Some careful thought will help us 'use' all this information productively.

Kautilya in the *Arthashastra* says it is very important for a person to be well-informed, but the important question is, why is this information required?

"Coming to know what is known, definite strengthening of what has become known, removal of doubt in case of two possible alternatives, finding out the rest in a matter that is partly known — this can be achieved with the help of ministers." (1.15.20-21)

Let us look at each aspect of 'information' separately:

- Realising What is Known

Some information we get, is already known to us. India's win in the cricket match could be direct information that you might have received while watching a live telecast. The same information may be repeated in the next day's newspapers. This information has very less value addition.

- Definite Strengthening of What Has Become Known

At times the information provided is half-baked. We are

not sure if it is correct. An additional information resource will help one understand if what is hearsay is correct, or not. We come to know that the director of a particular company has quit — this may not be correct information. It has to be cross-checked with the person who is directly working in that company.

- Removal of Doubt in Case of Two Possible Alternatives

Let us consider a situation where a hotel has been publicised as a 5-star property by its marketing team while the news is that it falls only in the 4-star category. There is a conflict of information. In that case, the right information, maybe from the hoteliers' association or from the tourism board's reports — will help one make the correct assessment.

- Finding Out the Rest in a Matter Partly Known

Most of the information floating around is not necessarily correct. They could be just gossips, rumours, and personal viewpoints. Therefore, it is essential to verify the facts and conduct research before we rush to make judgments. This is done by going to the primary source of the information rather than relying only upon secondary sources.

Most important — all information is really not required. One should be focused on what one wants. As Philip Kotler the marketing guru says, "Marketing research and market intelligence should give the information that *you* require, not what others want you to know."

54

Principles of Management

ALL MANAGEMENT THEORIES and concepts are based on certain principles. These essentials are the foundations with which we evaluate if the manager has been efficient, the organisation productive, and the objectives achieved. Today, management is not just a subject, but is also considered a science and an art.

But what exactly is management? How does one define management? Various voluminous books are available to answer this question. However, Kautilya has given the most refined view of management in a single verse, as short as five pointers in verse 42 of Chapter 15, of Book one of the *Arthashastra.*

Chanakya says, the basic elements of management are:

- The Means of Starting Undertakings (Assignments/ Projects)

When we say we have to manage, the question is what to manage? We need some project or assignment, in order to start acting upon it. Without a project, or an assignment, one cannot be called a manager. However, the best manager is the one who not only takes up a project given by his boss but instead 'creates' projects on his own. Stephen Covey in his book, *The Seven Habits of Highly Effective People*, describes this as 'proactiveness' — the highest quality of a good leader.

- The Excellence of Men and Materials

A manager has some resources, which can be used,

according to his discretion, to accomplish his tasks. They are the men who work under his direction and the tools that are used by him and these men. Hence, the other quality of a good manager is to make his men highly productive and ensure the optimum utilisation of materials like machinery, space, budgets etc given to them in order to reach the objectives.

- Deciding the Suitable Place and Time

Management is all about deciding the right place and right time to make our moves. Like in warfare, the timing is very crucial. When the enemy must be attacked, is not a question to be answered quickly. It requires careful planning, analysis, and also patience. This sense of the right 'timing' comes from one's own experience, knowledge, and also guidance from other sources.

- Provision Against Failure

Every move has to be carefully planned, taking into consideration two alternatives — the best case scenario (success) and the worst situation (total failure). Therefore, some kind of backup is required for every move. One needs to have alternative solutions ready in case of failure.

A businessman was once asked the secret of his success, for which he replied, "I take into consideration maximum failures at each stage. I plan the alternative moves even before I start the venture." It's like having Plan A, Plan B, and Plan C in place.

- Accomplishment of Work

Finally, management is all about getting 'results'. All said and done, at the end of the day, the achievement of results is what finally counts. It is very important to set a parameter to check if we have actually achieved what we set out for. That takes us to the first aspect of management — starting a project. Every project is started with a certain objective in mind. The process gets evolved and refined. But finally, the target has to be achieved even if the route taken to get there is different.

55

Keep an Open Mind

THE MIND IS LIKE A PARACHUTE — it works only when it is open. Some of the best business ideas come from listening to others.

Chanakya emphasises the importance of this point for various leaders,

"He should despise none, (but) should listen to the opinion of every one. A wise man should make use of the sensible words of even a child." (1.15.22)

A father was once watching his daughter play. She went to her mother and asked, "Mummy when will I get my new doll?", the mother replied, "It will take a few days, we will have to go to the shop which means we will have to travel for at least two hours."

Her father, who was thinking of a new business venture, realised the lack of a toy shop in their area. After a little bit of market research, he understood that, like them, all the parents in the area had to travel a long way to buy a toy for their children. He started a toy shop in the area and became a successful businessman.

One never knows where the next biggest idea will come from. The art of effective listening is very important in business. Even the most unexpected person could give you the key information and direction that you might have been waiting for, for years.

The following are some keys of effective listening.

- Despise None

One should be able to listen to every one without any preconceived notions. Politicians use this as their most effective tool to gather information at both, the top and the grassroots level. At one moment, they could be listening to investment proposals made by business tycoons, while the next moment they might be listening to the complaints of a local resident. Taking the total picture into consideration, they plan their next move.

Even a child's viewpoint is to be considered, as Kautilya said.

- Never React

At times, while listening to the opinion of others, it is tempting to say, "Oh, I already know that. I know it will not work." However, one should know how to control oneself. Cutting off a person while he is talking, is not just an insult to him, but will also end the possibilities of understanding the central message he is trying to convey.

Remember this, "The most important thing in communication is to hear what hasn't been said."

- Make Use of the Ideas

You may have the best ideas, but what is the use if you do not benefit from these ideas? Information is useless, unless it is applied for an effective purpose. Hence, we need to experiment with whatever we have understood. Successful businessmen are not those who just sit around and only think. They are men of dynamic action who are ready to take calculated risks and give their best to make an idea and plan work.

If you do not use your ideas, someone else surely will!

56

Managing Multiple Projects

EVERY LEADER, MANAGER, and executive has to handle multiple tasks at any given point of time. This is unavoidable. He may have been appointed for a particular work; however, with time, he will naturally get more and more responsibilities.

Management guru, Peter Drucker, in his book *On the Profession of Management*, is compassionate while describing the role of manager. He says, "The role of today's manager is very difficult. In any given situation, he has to handle multiple projects and assignments. He is always under pressure."

Kautilya, advises us on how to manage multiple projects and make more profits for the company;

"And (they) should bring about the commencement of what is not done, the carrying out of what is commenced, the improvement of what is being carried out and the excellence of (the execution of) orders, in the case of works." (1.15.51)

He looks at four types of works that an executive has to carry out:

- Commencement of What is Not Done

There are many things that need to be done. Good managers are those who start work on their own, rather than wait for the bosses to tell them what to do. Each person has to be proactive. He needs to build his own pipeline. New work has to be started. New experiments have to be tried. New techniques have to be applied.

- Carrying Out What Has Been Commenced

A project manager said it well, "It is not important how many projects I started, but how many I have completed." Everyone knows about pressure getting built up, simply because we are not able to complete the jobs we started. Procrastination is the worst disease. Once you pick up this bad habit, decisions are not taken on time, papers get piled up, and people lose focus. The best solution is the old adage, "What you ought to do tomorrow, do today, what you want to do today, do it now!"

- Improvement of What is Being Carried Out

One needs to ensure that the work started should end with high quality output. We should continuously strive for excellence. The core idea of the Japanese theory called Kaizen is that there is scope for continuous improvement in each task a person can do. Excellence then becomes a habit.

- Excellence in Execution of Orders

This means effective delegation. A manager, like all the other employees, has limited time and resources. Thus, in order to perform multiple tasking, he has to delegate some tasks to either his team members, or he must outsource some activities. Learning this art of effective delegation is very essential if one wants to climb up the corporate ladder. Management is not about only doing work on your own, but getting work done from others.

Once, a successful CEO who always seemed relaxed, was asked the secret of his cool temperament. He said, "Immediate decisions, faith in people whom I have given the work to, and spending more time in activities which will give us more money."

57

Politics and Politicians

'POLITICS IS DIRTY BUSINESS — it's not for me...'. Most of us run away from the very word. After all, politicians are commonly perceived to be selfish, corrupt, and totally manipulative.

This may be true to a great extent. But don't generalise. You can benefit a lot from 'good politicians', more than from management books. Leaders of various organisations, especially from the corporate world, can learn a lot from politicians about how to run an organisation.

Kautilya declares that a king who has not learnt politics is an unfit king,

"A king who has not learnt the teaching of the science of politics is unfit to listen to counsel." (1.15.61)

It means that such a leader will not be able to benefit from the advice and suggestions given to him.

For most people, reading this statement may come as a

shock. However, it is by learning politics that Chanakya himself became a mastermind. A master strategist, a great visionary, a kingmaker, Kautilya was also an expert in the science of politics, which made him an unparalleled statesman.

- Why Should a Corporate Leader Learn Politics?

Well, when you learn the science of politics, you will understand the way a politician thinks. A politician is one of the most powerful persons in society. If you want to understand power, understand politics.

- How Can We Learn Politics?

Know your local politicians. Not many people are even aware of the names of their corporator, MLA, or MP. When problems arise, they blame the system. But if you know your local politicians, then you can take the initiative by making a telephone call, filing a complaint, or even asking for a meeting with them.

- Keep an Open Mind

When meeting politicians, keep an open mind. You will learn more than you expected.

Politicians are wonderful resource managers, crowd-pullers, and team leaders. Since they move around a lot and deal with various levels of people in society, they are more aware of the problems faced by others, than a person sitting in the office knows.

- Learn Both Theory and Practice

One should also start reading the rules of political science from books. Such theories can be learnt from experts who have learnt 'academic politics', while the practical knowledge can be learnt from those occupying the all-powerful chair.

There is hardly any difference between the corporate world and the political world. It's all about power and authority. It's about dealing with the people. It's about how you can sail your ship in rough weather.

58

Constantly Educate Yourself

ALL OF US MUST HAVE, at some time or the other, heard people complaining about not getting 'deserved' promotions, or the boss not noticing their 'hard work'.

However, few realise that it is not the boss who is responsible for your growth in life, but the knowledge and the experience that *you* acquire. We need to continuously learn in order to grow. Only then will external benefits like increments, promotions, and higher responsibilities come to us.

Now, most believe that they do not get time to learn as they are fully occupied with work. So how will such 'busy' people learn new things?

This is where Kautilya advises us:

"During the remaining parts of the day and the night, he should learn new things and familiarise himself with those already learnt, and listen repeatedly to things not learnt." (1.5.15)

It is a very simple principle of time management. Utilise your evening and night hours to learn new things, instead of spending them on most unproductive things like partying, or other activities which are really meaningless.

Even in an office, the peak business hours are generally in the morning. The latter half of the day could, and should, be used meaningfully and effectively.

You may even use this time to ask questions and learn from seniors about processes that you have not fully understood.

Here are some tips on how you can use the second part of the day more effectively:

- Join a Class/Course

Today, there are various courses and classes conducted during post-office hours. Even MBA courses are offered for those who can attend evening classes. If you enroll for any such course, you will automatically leave the office on time.

- Read Books

Get into the habit of reading good books. Especially in a city like ours, you can effectively use your commuting time to do this. Choose the right books for learning new things. Do not just open any newspaper or magazine for the sake of passing time. You should read with a purpose.

- Meet the Right People

You should make it a point to meet at least two new people every week. They should be experts in their own field who know much more than you. Go to them with humility and learn the secret of their success.

All of this would, no doubt, make you a better man. After all, you would be following the old adage, "The only time well spent is the time spent learning new things!"

59

Disaster Management

WHY DO DISASTERS, OR CALAMITIES, happen? Well, who better to answer this question than the world's first management guru — Chanakya — who says,

"A calamity of a constituent, of a divine or human origin, springs from ill luck or wrong policy." (8.1.2)

So, whether we look at a state government, or a corporate entity, a calamity in any place or department always happens due to two reasons — ill luck, or wrong policy.

Ill luck is when a natural calamity occurs and is not in our control. Earthquakes, floods, forest fires, etc, might be predicted, but they certainly cannot be controlled, or avoided, fully.

However, the second type of calamity is man-made and happens due to mismanagement. Now, while these types of 'calamities' cannot be avoided, they can definitely be managed well.

But before we get into that, we need to ask ourselves why do human beings mismanage? Chanakya gives us the answer:

"Inversion of excellences, absence, a great defect, addiction, or affliction, constitutes a calamity." (8.1.3)

Let us look at each of them in detail:

- Inversion of Excellence

Simply put, it means 'not being excellent'. This happens when a manager is not proficient in his work. To avoid this, he has to be up-to-date with the latest developments in his own field. He should know both theory and practice, including the latest technical advances.

- Absence

If a person is absent on a regular and continuous basis, he will lose touch with what is happening at office. It is very necessary to take breaks from the work life. But, it is equally essential to get back into action once you are back to work. Every person should know how to switch off after a break and get back to work immediately.

- A Great Defect

Sometimes, a bad management team is the cause of calamities. People who are not qualified are placed at the helm. Or a bad decision-maker is made a leader due to the influence of his power. There could also be some personal defect in the leader which one may not be aware of. During high-pressure situations, such persons can't do anything. Worse, they run, blaming others if things go wrong.

- Addiction

Wine, women, wealth, and wielding power! Addictions to anything and everything will always ruin a leader's clarity of thinking. Therefore, throughout the *Arthashastra*, Chanakya emphasises that the king control his senses, only after controlling oneself can a leader control others.

- Affliction

It means causing pain and suffering to others. There are people who create unwanted and unnecessary problems to others. When in a position of power, a person should know how to use it for the benefit of others — not misuse it.

Therefore, it goes without saying that the first step towards effective disaster management is to select the right people, free from the above negative qualities.

60

Timing it Right

THERE IS A TIME FOR everything and everything has a time. Chankaya makes us understand this golden age-old rule by using a metaphor,

"The time of catching (elephants) is in the summer." (2.31.12)

This rule has to be understood by all those who run a business. Many businesses are seasonal and are dependent on various factors, for instance, tourism peaks during the vacation, and insurance and tax consultancy get more business during the months when returns are filed.

As we mature in our understanding of business, we get a better understanding of such cycles. Then the game becomes very easy to play. But how do we identify the 'right timing' in business? Here are some tips:

- Play the Game

When you do start a business, it is very hard initially to get a grip of all possible situations. Even if you are still unable to understand the rules of the game fully, please hit the ground running and play the game with the right spirit. You will mature with every fall.

Your mindset will change. You will get an insight into the way the industry works and will, eventually, end up at a much better place than where you started off from.

- Learn from Seniors

Every industry has businessmen who have played the game for longer than you have, and who know the cycles much better than you do. Seek shelter from them. Listen to their advice.

Try to have a godfather, a mentor or a guru who will not only guide you, but also allow you to make some mistakes. Having a guru means you are virtually safe with your experiments. He will never allow you to be a failure. Trust him. Your aim should be to become like him. As a senior corporate giant stated, "The best time of my life is when I sat at the feet of great masters and observed how they ran their businesses."

- Time Every Move

After the initial learning stages, you are prepared for the big war. In war, and in life, timing is the most critical element. No mistakes are allowed since you are now responsible not only for yourself, but also for the whole organisation.

Strategise, prioritise, plan and time every move — be it for marketing, or for launching a new product. As a leader, you have to be involved in the process — planning, executing and monitoring moves at every stage.

Business is all about preparing ourselves for the right time and opportunity. But remember — when the right time comes knocking at the door, we should not be sleeping inside.

61

Corporate Social Responsibility

THE CONCEPT OF Corporate Social Responsibility (CSR) is well-known throughout the business world today. It not only speaks of contributions made towards the benefit of the less privileged, but also calls for making oneself accountable to society.

Many think that CSR is a new concept. However, in our country, kings have been practising CSR for thousands of years. Even Kautilya's *Arthashastra* speaks about this.

He makes it clear, that, while it is the government's basic duty to maintain a society's well-being, even companies cannot stay away from this responsibility.

Referring to this issue, Chanakya had written,

"And those who are without relations have to be necessarily maintained." (1.12.1)

But how do businessmen practise these ideas? Here are a few tips:

- Take Responsibility

Dr. M.B. Atreya, a well-known management guru, had once said that we have to rise from CSR to PSR (Personal Social Responsibility). Each person has to personally commit to make his little contribution to improve the world around him. There are many things you can do — educate someone, plant a tree, support an artist, clean up the locality, etc.

- Contribute Money

Fund an already existing NGO project, or a spiritual organisation, this is the best way to start. You can even pool in the money. Collect a fund from the people interested. Then, every month, contribute the money collected to a project that you feel strongly about. There are many social projects that require funds. Find out about them on the Internet, but do not forget to check their authenticity, and only then make a contribution.

- Take Time Out

You just have to make time. Most of us always say that we do not have time, or that we are too busy. But it is important to shake off this mindset. Take time out once a week to do something for others.

- Don't Discourage Others

Under no circumstances should you underestimate this endeavour. Leaders are created when they see the problems of others. It's only then that they work towards solutions. In fact, the most important thing is that one should never discourage anyone who is performing some good deeds for the benefit of others.

The Chairman of a company had once decided to donate millions of dollars for handicapped children. During the board meeting, he was asked whether it was really worth donating such a huge amount for these children. He answered, "Yes it is, if one of them turns out to be your own child!"

62

A Stable Organisation

EVERYONE AIMS FOR THE GROWTH of their organisation — getting more projects and sales orders, increasing turnovers, and employing more people — are always the top priorities for business heads.

But, before we all begin to take the big leaps, we have to make sure that our foundation is strong and that we are stable within ourselves.

Chanakya says,

"The policy, following which he were to see neither the advancement nor the decline of his own undertakings, constitutes stable condition." (7.1.28)

What has been achieved, should not be lost. Even companies are now realising that, as they march ahead, their support system should be in place to conquer bigger markets. That's because it's important to keep your house in shape before you invite guests, or alliances.

- Financial Stability

Ensure that the cash flow into the organisation is regular and long-term. Outstandings have to be reduced. Collections from customers should be in time. A good banking and accounting system should be in place. Monitor finance reports regularly to keep an eye on these.

- People Stability

A company may be getting more orders, but what's the use if existing employees are shifting jobs? Stability of people has to be ensured. It's a major challenge to all HR heads that, before they recruit new people, their existing ones should not leave. It's a case of ensuring that the bucket you are filling with water has no hole in the bottom.

- Learning Stability

It's the world of knowledge-workers now. It's important for everyone to maintain a steady search for knowledge. Continuous innovation and upgrading is the secret of success of all great companies. The decline starts when one thinks he knows it all. Learn from others and your own experiences.

- Vision Stability

To fulfill the above requirements, a stable vision is very important. Before anyone starts an organisation, it's important to have a clear vision and a mission. If the company's sole motive is only to earn profits, the future is going to be dark. It is also important to impart the vision of the leader to every single employee to inspire them to work hard. Only when the 'inspiration' is maintained will the organisation grow.

You have to always remember to think about the long-term, instead of the short-term. Our Indian scriptures use two words to indicate this. *Shreyas* — the path of the good, which is initially difficult, but the person who selects it emerges as a winner at the end. *Preyas* — the path of the wrong, which initially seems comforting, but ruins us in the future. So, just take a deep breath, choose the right path and keep walking…

63

Working in New Regions

THE NEED FOR EXPANSION and growth is universal. Like humans, even corporations want to grow. Companies want to introduce new products, explore new markets, and grow in their turnover. But when a company wants to expand into new territory, it has to send people into the region first.

For such people who are sent out to make new discoveries, Chanakya suggests that the company take full responsibility of them in the unexplored region:

"He should provide one making a new settlement with grains, cattle, money, and other things." (5.2.4)

When a company sets its sights on a new region, it has to send one of its trusted seniors to go there and settle down for some time. The cost of this and their safety, has to be ensured. How does the leader do that?

- Do Your Research Well

Whenever a company wants to expand — whether for a new market, for acquiring another firm, or even making a strategic alliance — a lot of research has to be done. Reading, getting the information from industrial reports and consultants, etc is essential. Also, talk to a local person to give you further insights. This is the basic foundation for expansion.

- Send a Pilot Team

Based on the information gathered, send one or more members from your senior management to that region.

Cross-verification of the facts gathered is essential. Meet lots of people — from various backgrounds — to understand the region, and its culture, better. Your 'eyes' and 'ears' are the basic tools for this. Document your study and, after you get back, present it to the parent company.

- Plan Your Move in Phases

If the venture seems profitable, move in phases. Have you ever observed how the various multinationals make their entry into India? Usually, a single person will move in first and stay in the region for about a year or two. During this phase, Chanakya advises that the firm handle the entire costs of living and security of the person. Some firms even move entire families of their representatives here, taking care of their children's education, vacations, and entertainment.

- Become Fully Operational

After gaining a year or two of experience, one will get a grip of the new region. Then move into full-operation mode and succeed in it. Note that it is not about conquering a new territory — a company also has to be socially responsible. Make sure you also 'contribute' to the new place instead of just making profits and taking it away from there.

Swami Ishwaranandaji of Chinmaya Mission put it best when he said, "Conquering does not mean killing. It means taking a place in the hearts of the newly acquired region."

64

Intelligence Management

SINCE OUR ANCIENT INDIAN and traditional management books are based on sound principles, they have always had a lot of depth. This is the reason they have survived the test of time. Even today, readers write in with queries on the relation these age-old books have with today's world.

Well, they are in august company.

Being in the field of corporate training and strategic management consulting, I have also been asked by various directors, CEOs, and chairmen — "What's so special about Chanakya (or Kautilya) and his book *Arthashastra* that makes it so relevant even in the modern business world?"

Now, this is a very interesting question for all those who want to study and practise the pearls of wisdom gleaned from the *Arthashastra.*

Here are two very strong reasons that make *Kautilya's Arthashastra* an eternal masterpiece, and Chanakya himself an unforgettable legend:

- A Subject Called 'Aanveekshikee'

One of the most striking features of the *Arthashastra* is that it is a very logical book. Before studying this book, kings had to go through a foundation course to prepare them for the higher knowledge of politics. In *Arthashastra* itself, Chanakya suggests that a student who wants to master this book should first study a subject called

Aanveekshikee. This Sanskrit terminology is very hard to translate, but the nearest word in English could be 'Logic'. So Chanakya calls for a student's ability in logical thinking to be developed first and foremost.

Aanveekshikee is a very interesting subject, but hardly known to our generation. It is a mixture of logical, lateral, alternative, analytical, and out-of-the-box thinking. In short, we can call it 'the science of thinking'. It helps a person develop his IQ and converts him into a strategist.

Therefore, *Arthashastra* can be said to be a book on 'Intelligence Management'. Once this ability sharpens your intelligence, you will be able to handle higher responsibilities.

- A Foundation in Spirituality

The second strong factor in favour of the *Arthashastra* is that it tells leaders to inculcate an in-depth spirituality.

Why? Because, in the end, leaders have to deal with power and powerful persons. Power can corrupt, and absolute power can corrupt absolutely.

Therefore, to prevent the misuse of power, Chanakya suggests a study of the Vedas and other philosophical books. Thus, he attempts to create persons who will become value-based leaders. After all, a man is what he does in the dark when no one is watching him. Only a selfless leader can serve others properly.

Always remember that everyone is gifted with some intelligence. But hardly anyone is taught to 'manage' their intellect. And everyone may seem to be spiritual, but rarely do leaders of position take spiritual-based decisions coupled with logical insight.

Now, the *Arthashastra* guarantees both and is, therefore, an eternal book of management.

65

Organisational Planning

THE INVENTION OF THE CALENDAR is a very important landmark in the history and development of mankind. It helps us track time and document the various events of the past. It tells us our present conditions and also helps forecast, predict, and plan for the future.

Can you ever spend a single day without knowing the date, or even the time? We would not only get confused ourselves, but also end up confusing all those around us.

Therefore, time-keeping instruments like the calendar are very important tools of reference in our lives.

Chanakya also used the calendar as a basis for time-management:

"The royal year, the month, the paksha, the day, the dawn (vyushta), the third and seventh pakshas of (the seasons such as) the rainy season, the winter season, and the summer short of their days, the rest complete, and a separate intercalary month are (the divisions of time)." (2.6.12)

In the above verse, one is able to see the periods factored in for planning. Some of these are still good for organisational planning today:

- Annual Planning

Here, the goals for the year are set and the road-maps are

prepared too. Strategies and polices are factored in to achieve the same. Usually, Annual General Meetings (AGM) are organised to inform all members of a team about these targets.

If need be, new teams are formed and new job profiles are defined to meet the set objectives. AGMs also help one take stock of the previous year's performance.

- Seasonal Planning

Everything has a season and there is a season for everything — this is nature's law. Once we understand this, it's easy to look at the ups and downs of any plan.

After all, you will never find a farmer expecting his fruits to be produced the same day he has planted the seeds. He knows he has to wait patiently for the right season after carrying out the required duties.

Even in business, there are trends and seasons. Mature businessmen factor them into their long-term planning. For example, in India, maximum purchases occur during festival seasons.

Consider the recent Diwali season — every single person knows that the last festive week must have resulted in the bloated sales of every product in the market.

- Planning for Rest

One may work throughout the year, but it's important to rest from time to time so that we can work more effectively. Chanakya suggests the need to plan for rest too, in any organisation. I know of companies where, during the beginning of the year itself, all the employees plan their annual leave and apply for it.

In most European companies, it's compulsory to take a

one-month annual leave for rest and for re-energising oneself.

A good organisational plan consists of a mix of long-term planning (five-year, ten-year, or even twenty five-year plans) and short-term planning (monthly, weekly, and daily plans).

The top management focuses on the broad framework while others focus on the nuts and bolts of the business. Together, their combined and time-managed work would ultimately better the future of the firm itself.

66

The Best and the Better

A GREAT THINKER ONCE SAID, "If I were to create something new, I would study all that is best and make my product even better." About 2,400 years ago, Chanakya himself applied this law.

The very first verse of *Kautilya's Arthashastra* says:

"This single treatise (Kautilya's Arthashastra) on the science of politics has been prepared mostly by bringing together the teachings of as many treatises on the science of politics as have been composed by ancient teachers for the acquisition and protection of the earth." (1.1.1)

Did you know that there were at least fourteen other *Arthashastras* prior to the one written by Chanakya?

The masters of the past were not afraid to accept that innovation and creativity started by learning from others, and even gave credit where it was due, like in Chanakya's case in the above verse.

But there are certain steps for doing this:

- What Do You Want to Achieve?

First, our destination has to be clear. Define this and half the battle is won. When Ratan Tata first announced that he will bring out a Rs 1-lakh car, it showed clarity of purpose. The rest followed. If you are a businessman, think about the product, or service, you want to offer. If you are an artist, what will you create? If you are a player, where and which medal do you want to win? Remember Gandhiji's words — "Find a purpose, the means will follow."

- How Will You Do It?

You have to start the journey immediately after setting a goal. How? Well, Chanakya had said we should learn from the best that is already available. Do some research, read books by an expert in your field, study or join a course. Be sure about why you want to re-invent the wheel! And the key word is 'improve'. So learn from the best. If you are a swimmer, and aim to win an Olympic medal, you'd better get trained by the world's best swimmers. This will help you achieve the goal faster.

- When Will You Finish?

Now that you are ready to learn from the best, set a deadline for yourself — the time by when you will reach your goal, converting your study and training into success. This deadline will help you move with extra speed. When the American President first announced that a man would land on the moon and safely return to earth within a decade, it was a definite deadline. And the scientists achieved it! Chanakya followed the above steps too. That's the reason his *Arthashastra* has become an immortal book.

Now it's your turn to create something immortal too.

67

Time Management

ALL OF US ARE LIVING in an extremely fast world now, with a dire need for effective time-management. But one can always learn from Chanakya's centuries-old *Arthashastra.* According to him, being mindful of what we have to do is the biggest tip for managing time well.

Chanakya had said:

"Thus, he (superintendent of cattle) should be cognizant of the number of animals." (2.29.15)

Cognizant means being aware or mindful of one's responsibilities, and being in control of them. Hence, in this line, Chanakya says that, at any given point of time, the head of the cattle department should know the exact number of cattle his people are handling.

We can also use this verse to guide us in our daily activities:

- Understand Your Goals

The first step in time-management is to know where you want to reach, and by when. Most of us are running without an agenda, or clarity of purpose. Always question yourself — Why am I doing this? Am I supposed to do this? What results am I going to get by doing this activity? Many of us do not know our job profiles properly. If you are not sure, ask your boss, and be clear about his expectations. Make a list of the roles that you play — department head, team leader, project in-charge, parent, child, etc. Then, under each role, write your responsibilities and prioritise them.

- Note Everything

When you are in the midst of your regular work, there can be various interruptions. Some are external disturbances, while others created by your own mind. Phone calls, a new idea, a bill that you had forgotten to pay — all these are common distractions. Such events disturb our current work flow.

At such times, note your thoughts down immediately on a sheet of paper, or even on your mobile, or computer. Then you will not forget it. Your mind will be at peace. Then, after making the note, continue doing your current work at hand, if that is your priority.

- Check Your List Regularly

When you are free, look at the list you have made and act on each item. A busy manager once said, "I look at my to-do list at least a dozen times each day. It constantly reminds me of what I have to do, and I accordingly make time for it in my busy schedule."

The moment you have finished some work, make a note in a relevant file or folder. This can be useful when you prepare your reports. It's all about being "...cognizant of the number of animals."

Just keep in mind that all this advice can be useful only if one is self-disciplined. No amount of 'book knowledge', or time-management courses will help if you get carried away by the urgent matters 'others' bring.

68

Ensuring Growth

BEING AN EXPERT IN the field of *Rajniti* (statesmanship), Chanakya could communicate exactly what a leader (king) is expected to do to ensure the growth of his kingdom.

He had said:

"There is no country without people, and no kingdom without a country." (13.4.5)

Here, 'country' stands for the rural villages, or the 'countryside'. In other words, Chanakya stresses on the interdependence of people, villages, and the kingdom they form together, and the attention each needs for overall growth. The same law can be applied to any institution, or organisation, as well:

- People: Customers and Clients

Can any company survive without its clients or customers? Their needs have to be fulfilled by the company's products and services. So these have to be improved. But remember that the word 'people' here also applies to the employees and the managers who run the organisation. They also have to be taken care of, or there will be a disaster as no one would be ready to cater to the clients.

- Country: The Market

A large number of clients and customers grouped together in a particular region are called a market. Understanding the demand and supply ratio of any market is of prime importance. The company has to focus on this aspect of business.

Additionally, with all markets being dynamic and ever-changing, a company's sales and marketing department will have to stay on top of, as well as predict, these changes to stay ahead of competitors.

- Kingdom: The Company

People and the country come together to form the kingdom, or a company in today's corporate world. Remove either of the two and the company will disappear. If a company has to grow, it has to expand its current markets. This is what growth planning is.

Any person who wants to build a good marketing strategy should understand this rule. Study individual customers to understand market issues. Based on that, refine your products and services. Then understand the need of different markets and customise your products accordingly.

In this manner, the firm's leader will be able to keep his customers happy and, in turn, increase market capitalisation and make the company grow faster into a truly globalised organisation.

69

Land as an Alternative Asset

OWNING PROPERTY HAS BECOME a key investment for many people. In rural areas, land translates into the very existence of a person. Indeed, property is eternally named in that age-old formulation of the prime requirements for survival — *Roti*, *Kapda*, aur *Makaan*.

But here, the onus is on food, clothing, and, property, rather than shelter. Chanakya had stressed this centuries ago in the *Arthashastra*:

"Of the excellence of land, affording shelter is best." (7.11.22)

He had even listed many ideas on how to select land, or property, based on its qualities — conducive to agriculture, having a perennial source of water, rich in minerals, etc.

However, as in the verse above, he preferred that land which gives us shelter during tough times. Now, how do people like us, who stay in cities, apply this?

- Purchase Land in Smaller Places

Having a property in Mumbai is a dream. It's one of the costliest cities in the world. If you are among the lucky ones who already have a house in Mumbai, or in another similarly big city, do not stop there.

Purchase a small property in a smaller place as an additional shelter and investment. Why? Simple — if you can build one home in a metro city, it shows you have the capability for creating more, and you should do exactly that as an alternative to your residence.

- Build and Use It

Now do not just purchase a piece of land and let it lie waste. Build a house on it. Use it from time to time. There are many whom I know who own houses in their villages and small towns, but never use it. Someone else does.

It's important you stay there at least twice a year. Thus, you will get used to a different place. God forbid, in case you have to leave your current city, it will be an easy migration for you.

- It's Security

We never know what the future has in store for us. However, we can at least have a back-up plan for shelter and survival. If a natural calamity hits our city, at least we can fall back on a reverse migration of sorts. In spite of problems that may crop up, we can say — "At least I have a house for shelter. Let me start again."

This would especially help in times of economic crises, such as the recession that affected the world in 2008-09.

Chanakya's strategy was always to "...predict the unpredicted, and prepare an alternative." Your additional land or property can be this alternative.

70

Crime Planners

AFTER THE TERROR ATTACKS IN MUMBAI on 26/11, every citizen was angry. The international community also took these attacks seriously and lent its support. So now that Qasab, the sole surviving terrorist, has been sentenced to death, it is important for Pakistan to arrest some of the biggest masterminds behind such attacks. How do we punish the criminals after they have been caught?

Chanakya gave us his view in *Arthashastra*:

"He who causes another to commit an act of force saying, 'I shall accept responsibility', shall be punished double." (3.17.11)

In other words, according to Chanakya, those who force (or brainwash) others into committing a crime are more responsible for the consequences. Their punishment should be double of what is faced by those actually executing the crime.

Young boys like Qasab and the other terrorists who executed their masters' plans were just a small part of the deadly show. Now that we are being led to the bigger planners, we have to tackle them:

- At the Top Level

A strong initiative must be taken by our government, as well the international community and the United Nations, so that this issue is dealt with far more seriously. This top level initiative should continue. The fight is till the finish.

So all the powerful — and responsible — authorities have to ensure that the results of their endeavours are much more better and fruitful than ever before. Timely execution of their plans is more important than mere academic analysis.

- At the Corporate Level

The attacks showed how even business organisations are now on the terror radar. Corporates like the Tatas and the

Oberoi group were directly impacted. So the events of November 26, 2008, should always remind us that avoiding terrorism is not just the government's responsibility.

Companies have to take care of their employees — both need each other in equal manner in such times. The corporate leaders especially should communicate their concerns and issues to their employees and solve all security problems together.

- At the Individual Level

As I said already, one has to appreciate the way the fire is still in the hearts of our citizens. No individual should ever forget these incidents.

If you cannot participate, at least keep the momentum going by signing petitions, forwarding mails and voicing your opinion in some way.

JAICO PUBLISHING HOUSE

Elevate Your Life. Transform Your World.

ESTABLISHED IN 1946, Jaico Publishing House is home to world-transforming authors such as Sri Sri Paramahansa Yogananda, Osho, the Dalai Lama, Sri Sri Ravi Shankar, Sadhguru, Robin Sharma, Deepak Chopra, Jack Canfield, Eknath Easwaran, Devdutt Pattanaik, Khushwant Singh, John Maxwell, Brian Tracy, and Stephen Hawking.

Our late founder Mr. Jaman Shah first established Jaico as a book distribution company. Sensing that independence was around the corner, he aptly named his company Jaico ('Jai' means victory in Hindi). In order to service the significant demand for affordable books in a developing nation, Mr. Shah initiated Jaico's own publications. Jaico was India's first publisher of paperback books in the English language.

While self-help, religion and philosophy, mind/body/spirit, and business titles form the cornerstone of our non-fiction list, we publish an exciting range of travel, current affairs, biography, and popular science books as well. Our renewed focus on popular fiction is evident in our new titles by a host of fresh young talent from India and abroad. Jaico's recently established translations division translates selected English content into nine regional languages.

Jaico distributes its own titles. With its headquarters in Mumbai, Jaico has branches in Ahmedabad, Bangalore, Chennai, Delhi, Hyderabad, and Kolkata.

SINCE 1946